# The Lives Around Us

## Daily Meditations for Nature Connection

# The Lives
# Around Us

Daily Meditations for Nature Connection

Dan Papworth

Easterlich 2018

CHRISTIAN
ALTERNATIVE

Winchester, UK
Washington, USA

First published by Christian Alternative Books, 2016
Christian Alternative Books is an imprint of John Hunt Publishing Ltd.,
Laurel House, Station Approach,
Alresford, Hants, SO24 9JH, UK
office1@jhpbooks.net
www.johnhuntpublishing.com
www.christian-alternative.com

For distributor details and how to order please visit the 'Ordering' section on our website.

Text copyright: Dan Papworth 2015

ISBN: 978 1 78535 256 0
Library of Congress Control Number: 2015956010

A CIP catalogue record for this book is available from the British Library.

Design: Stuart Davies

Printed and bound by CPI Group (UK) Ltd, Croydon, CR0 4YY, UK

We operate a distinctive and ethical publishing philosophy in all areas of our business, from our global network of authors to production and worldwide distribution.

# CONTENTS

Acknowledgements     x

Introduction     1

1. Ash – the tree of life     8
2. Red Ant – encountering the 'other'     11
3. Badger – digging deeper     14
4. Raven – the incredible reach of God     18
5. St George's Mushroom – the life within     23
6. Rook – prophecy, protection and the sharing of wisdom     29
7. Brown Trout – celebrating diversity     33
8. Magpie – peace and trust in the face of uncertainty     39
9. Peregrine – life in all its fulness     43
10. Water Vole – focussing on what is essential     47
11. Common Frog – rediscovering familiar paths     50
12. Shrew – God's surprising choice     54
13. Blackbird – the way of the artist     57
14. Roe Deer – integrating feminine and masculine     63
15. High Brown Fritillary – the slow work of God     69
16. Leopard Slug – an unlikely friend     73
17. Rosebay Willowherb – life on the margins     77
18. White-berried Mistletoe – truth hidden in plain sight     82
19. Honey Bee – complexity, cooperation, communication and congruence     86
20. Pipistrelle – embracing our shadow     90
21. Ivy – joyfulness in creation     93
22. Grey Seal – listening to the heart     98
23. Red Squirrel – vulnerability, resilience and playful learning     103
24. Stoat – anger, confrontation and resolution     107
25. Common Toad – born of the Spirit     110

26. Trees – wise guardians of time     115
27. Hawthorn – suffering and endurance     117
28. Hedgehog – being known and being loved     121
29. Jay – mindfulness and symbiosis     127
30. Mole – the power of solitude and reticence     129
31. Kingfisher – setting our eyes upon the goal     134
32. Mayfly – celebrating all we have     138
33. Common Orb Weaver – entrusting the future to God     143
34. Meteorite – the deep silence of the Ancient of Days     147
35. Fox – awareness of self and environment     151
36. Adder – facing our depths     158
37. Chicken of the Woods – looking at the heart     163
38. Oak – the gift of true community     168
39. Common Hermit Crab – embracing change     173
40. Eel – knowing our true home     179

Conclusions     185
Notes     196
Websites and further reading     205
Scripture Index     212

**Illustrations by Stu McLellan**
Totem     7
Badger Spoor     38
St Georges Mushroom     68
Brown Trout     97
Honey Bee     126
Jay's Feather     157
Oak Leaf     184
Surrounding     195

For Edwin and Marie, who taught me to walk; and Sarah, who walks with me.

# Acknowledgements

This is not quite my first writing project but it has been the most intensive so far and I now know why so many authors thank their spouses and families. Sarah gave me the gift of time and kept me grounded, consistently putting her unique combination of love and practicality at my service, generously extending herself for the sake of my spiritual growth. Joel and Ethan had little say in the matter, but simply by being themselves they continue to give me gift upon gift. Exhibiting delight and contemplation, playfulness, openness and sensitivity, in the discipline of nature connection they are so often my most able tutors. My parents, Edwin and Marie Papworth, continue to delight in me and give every kind of encouragement I could wish for. I will always be grateful that I was introduced to walking, and therefore nature, from such a young age. In Stu McLellan I found a true artist who, with soul and skill, has beautifully and yet so simply captured with his illustrations something of the spirit and presence of the creatures in this book. Bruce Stanley and Steve Hollinghurst were immediately positive and practical in equal measure, generous with their time, and honest in both praise and criticism, enabling me to benefit from their combined experience as writers of note. Bruce, along with Matt Cole, also gifted me with a chance to go deeper into the life of Roe Deer by inviting me to co-lead two workshops with Verity Peacock at the Greenbelt Festival in 2015. I am grateful to Lin Ball for her honesty and practical advice; Noel Moules for his warm support, generosity of spirit and passion for nature; Stewart Manegold, who reminded me on more than one occasion to listen to the heart; Pete Barbour for his help with some of the images; and Dr John Bimson and Dr Knut Heim for helping me with my Hebrew and signposting me to further reading on this important subject. Special thanks are due to those at John Hunt Publishing who worked with me on this project: Maria Barry, Matthew Cashmore, Stuart Davies, Mary Flatt, Trevor Greenfield, Catherine Harris, Dominic James, Maria Moloney, Denise Smith and Nick Welch. I am grateful to HarperCollins for having such a generous "gratis" policy in relation to the New Revised Standard Version of the Bible. Thanks also to the many Forest Church people who read some of the early drafts and gave so much positive feedback. I owe so much to so many people – far too many to name – who have influenced me in my journey as a Christian, and those with whom I have dialogued over the past few years. Thanks to Connie Jenth, Olly Ward, Seb Ward, Cate Williams, Howard Williams and Seren Williams and everyone in the growing community that is Cheltenham Forest Church for being part of this journey. I am also grateful to *Facebook*, *Twitter* and *Wordpress*, all of whom have enabled conversations that could not have happened otherwise. They have been instrumental in my explorations for at least the past two years, probably longer. Finally, I would like to express my appreciation and gratitude to the creatures who grace these pages and who not only make life possible but enrich it beyond imagining.

Believe me, as one who has experience,

you will find much more among the woods than ever you will among books.

Woods and stones will teach you what you can never hear from any master.

– Bernard of Clairvaux (1090-1153), *The Letters* (London: Barnes and Oates, 1958) p.156

# Introduction

There are some lovely moments in the Gospels in which Jesus, sitting or walking with his disciples, calls their attention to something. There is a sense that the disciples inhabit two worlds but are perhaps aware only of one until he says to them "Do you see this?" and, looking more closely, something deeper is revealed. Approaching nature in our own time we too find that we occupy two worlds, those of science and spirituality. Most people today seem more familiar with the first but long to experience more of the second. It was not so very long ago that people understood Nature to be a living thing, much more than a mere mechanism obeying unchanging laws, and ourselves as part of it rather than separate from it. So this is an attempt to bring knowledge and spirit into closer companionship. Coming from the Christ tradition,[1] having studied Environmental Science, I do not believe there is an inherent conflict, even if in the past they have seemed like "two countries separated by a common language".[2] For many centuries Christians have broadly accepted the belief that nature may be seen as a kind of book that, like the Bible, contains revelation. Indeed Scripture itself seems to point this way. The God we believe in does not belong to some other realm but has very firmly chosen this one. So it made sense to me to begin by setting these two perspectives alongside each other, like companions walking in the woods, in the knowledge that they are bound to speak and, in you, find out where that conversation leads.

## Watching our steps

As with any exploration we need to look where we are going. Humans are great storytellers, and the experiences of many generations and cultures has furnished us with stories featuring those creatures with whom we share the natural world. In recent

1

generations a new awareness has begun to emerge as we ask "who is telling this story and to whom?" And of course we find that humans are telling the stories to other humans. In fact our fellow creatures are quite alien to us. So I want to be wary of the tendency to observe a particular characteristic in a fellow creature and draw too obvious a parallel with human behaviours. I want to avoid common myths (for example, "the solitary badger") that have no basis in fact, to recognise the 'otherness' of our fellow creatures, and let them teach us. So I have done my best here, but there is a long way to go. Bruce Stanley, author of *Forest Church*[3] once commented that he would not feel confident to make big statements about all trees, and is not sure how long he would need to stay with just one solitary Birch before he could confidently claim to know it.[4] This diffidence is a valuable counterpoint to the brazen confidence with which humans have tramped into the woods in the past. We need to learn to tread lightly, but the good news is that we do have a place. We do not need to carve it out. Nature is hospitable to all.

Each short chapter begins with a reflection on a specific creature, almost all of them native to the British Isles. I am not seeking to be comprehensive but rather thought-provoking, so if something piques your interest, trust that instinct and research further. With the Bible readings (quotations are from the New Revised Standard Version) my suggestion is that you read slowly, asking for the grace of awareness, and see whether any particular word or phrase stands out for you. For copyright reasons I am a little limited in how much I am allowed to quote, so you may want to have your own Bible alongside, if you have one. Build some time of silence into your daily routine and, if something resonates within you stay with it, asking for deeper insight. In most, but not quite all, of the chapters I include some steps we can take to aid the creature mentioned, based on the belief that there is plenty of room in this country for everyone. "Love your neighbour" and even "love your enemy" applies here, just as it does towards other humans.[5] The prayer section is a suggestion not a prescription, and the same is true for any exercises. These things are offered to help you but if the Spirit leads you in another way then trust that instinct. There is plenty of time to come back to any of this if you wish. I am also aware that it may not be realistic to do an exercise on the day appointed, and some engage with emotions you may not be feeling right then (most of us don't have our feelings 'on tap'). The key is to do what is right for you, to be kind to yourself. Allow yourself to be loved and see how that love transforms you.

It is strange what stays with you over the years. I recall a field trip during my first degree (Environmental Science at the University of Plymouth) when a fellow student put in a word for common English names on the basis that they are more poetic and descriptive than those favoured by science. The use of Latin names takes us into the realm of taxonomy, a discipline that seeks to categorize and create hierarchies as well as establish relationships. Whilst this may be useful for research, I agree that it can lack soul and so I have chosen to use common names throughout my text. If this is an irritant to tidier minds than mine I apologise, but life is not tidy, and human attempts to impose order are all too often energy-intensive and even damaging. Let a thousand flowers bloom!

There is an ongoing debate about introducing new, genderless, pronouns into the English language, something that would resolve a big difficulty I had in writing this. The problem is that, whilst some creatures divide neatly into female and male, others do not. Some are hermaphrodite (containing both sexes), others are effectively genderless. I want to show respect to my subjects, all of whom are living creatures, not objects, so in each chapter I have chosen to use the words "he" and "she" and never "it". This does not mean that I am excluding the other sex, but rather suggesting we focus in on an imagined individual, where appropriate, as we contemplate the life of another. Since the suggested alternatives (zhe, ze, xe, co, e) are not yet in common use, I have decided not to use them. I just think it would distract from the text. So whilst I am aware that saying "he" of a Hawthorn tree, which always carries both sexes in "his" flowers, is inadequate and even a bit misleading, I have decided to press ahead and I ask you to bear with me. You will see that, for the sake of balance, I use male and female in different chapters but within each chapter I have maintained consistency, again to avoid confusion.

I owe a great deal to all sorts of people for the information and insights that are posted online. However, since this is not primarily an academic work, it did not feel appropriate to reference every statement. Where there is an original point I have cited the source, and occasionally I quote verbatim when I do not believe I could put something better. Most of the facts I present about the creatures in these pages can be said to be in the public domain, and with this kind of information I have not bothered to cite the source. Where I have put a reference you may assume that other information in the same chapter has also come from one of those sources. It is of course possible that I am reproducing information that is not quite accurate. I have done my best to crosscheck but nobody is perfect. Any factual errors herein are mine and I am happy to be corrected. I strongly believe that there is no conflict between the world of faith and the real world. This is the world God created, so the more we know about it, the better. My only caveat to that is that information needs to be ethically obtained.

## The praise of the creatures

During the writing of this book I have been interested to see the reactions of people I have talked to about it. Most immediately get the starting point: that the world can instruct us about God. They also accept that there is no conflict between the Bible and creation, the two books of God, and that this kind of exploration is relatively new and uncharted. But it is amazing how hard people find it to let go of the idea that other creatures are somehow here for our benefit and use. I would like to suggest that the mole was not made for us. He has a life of his own. He is not a resource for us to utilise, he is not there for our amusement or our education. He is not a commodity. Yes I can usefully learn about him because he is my neighbour and, as his neighbour, I have certain responsibilities, but the first of these is to build trust and respect. There are very few creatures on planet Earth that fail to respect us. Isn't it time we developed the same maturity?

It has been said that, unlike humans, other species in the world offer praise to their creator not through specific acts of worship but merely by being themselves (see Psalms 19, 104 and 148). My own sense is that any attempt to differentiate humanity from 'the rest' of nature creates more problems than it solves. We are intimately linked with other species, from the microbes that inhabit our bodies to the macrobes we eat, observe, wonder at and occasionally flee from. We have no life independently of other life. Yes, it may be accepted that modern science, which emerged from the eighteenth century onwards, has discovered many things that have benefitted us, not least because of its tendency to dissect and categorize. But in these days we have become more aware of the damage this does to us, and a new appreciation of our interdependence is being sought. We are part of a larger phenomenon that is life, and the discovery is a joyful one. Perhaps our own ongoing reflection and prayer can reveal to us just how fully our own being expresses praise. My hope is that this book will enable you to be more fully yourself and thereby to give greater praise to your creator.

There are, of course, a number of creatures with which we are familiar, or at least we think we are: Fox, Badger, Owl, Deer all make an appearance – predictably enough, you might think. But I have attempted to incorporate some species that would not necessarily make the 'A-list'. I have done this because I really want to call these preferences into question, to heighten awareness of how and why we turn away from some things and towards others, and to encourage you to value, and enter into a deeper relationship with, creatures you may not have previously considered. So the journey, I hope, will not be an entirely comfortable one as unhelpful scripts are rewritten. It may not be a road completely untravelled before – I am relying heavily on the discoveries of others – but I hope it will, for many, be a new road, one not previously taken.

Dan Papworth, February 2015

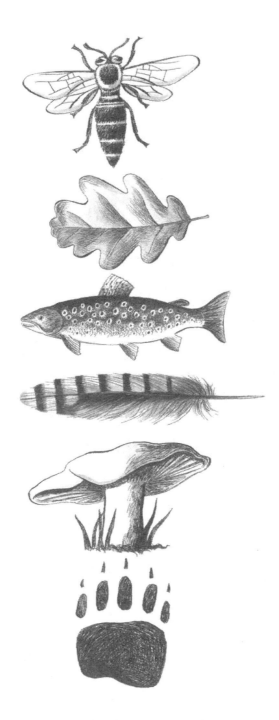

## Chapter 1

# Ash – the tree of life

In Norse mythology the cosmos is held together by a single, eternally green Ash tree: Yggdrasil, the "world tree", also called the Tree of Life. In Britain, the Ash makes up around 5 per cent of our woodlands, but she plays host to around 45 other species which depend upon her.[6]

In our own time Ash has come under threat from a fungal disease named, straightforwardly if rather obviously, "Ash Dieback". On dry days at eye level you can spot the symptoms:[7] brown or black staining on the leaf stalks, stem discolouration (the classic symptom is a small section of brown or purple in the middle of an otherwise healthy, olive green, stem) and diamond-shaped cracks (lesions) in the bark. The terrible loss of this country's elms from the late 1960s onwards is still within living memory. Indeed I was born just after the worst of it and I remember the feeling with which one of my primary school teachers described what had happened. So it was with very mixed emotions that I discovered the large mature tree in our neighbour's garden, which dominates the view from my children's bedroom windows, is an Ash. Some people may think it strange to pray for the well-being of a tree, but all things are related. It may even be that the death of these beautiful trees is yet another invitation to live in greater harmony with the environment that is our home. The Ash teaches us that age and vitality are not opposites, and that life can be both robust and fragile.

Find out where the Ash trees are in your area and monitor them for signs of dieback. If you see the symptoms report it immediately to the Forestry Conmmission (there is even an App for this: see their website, which is also listed at the end of this book). The healthiest place for Ash is not in dense stands but amongst other trees. This is actually true for most species – it is only humans who like to create monocultures and then spend huge amounts of energy and resources fighting the diseases that inevitably follow. If you want to do something really ambitious then why not purchase a woodland with some friends and manage it as a "coppice with standards"? This ancient practice yielded a continuous supply of useful wood for communities in the past. It provides a rich habitat for a number of struggling native species of plants and animals and will be the healthiest playground your children will ever know.

## From Genesis 2:9 (NRSV)

*Out of the ground the Lord God made to grow every tree that is pleasant to the sight and good for food, the tree of life also in the midst of the garden, and the tree of the knowledge of good and evil.*

## From Revelation 22:1-2 (NRSV)

*Then the angel showed me the river of the water of life, bright as crystal, flowing from the throne of God and of the Lamb through the middle of the street of the city. On either side of the river is the tree of life with its twelve kinds of fruit, producing its fruit each month; and the leaves of the tree are for the healing of the nations.*

## For reflection and prayer

Is the tree of life in Genesis and Revelation an Ash tree? We do not know and it does not really matter, but the green, healthy vitality of this tree has long stood for the youth and energy of God who, far from being an old man on a cloud (where does that image come from anyway?), is eternally young and invites us to eternal life. For many people today "eternity" is an unattractive prospect. "It could go on a bit, couldn't it?" one of my family members recently quipped. But what if eternity, rather than being a long time, is the experience of living fully in the present? To what extent do I live either in the past or in the future, neither of which is ever truly satisfying? Can I understand the present moment as the place where I am called and the place where God is to be found? Speaking of the Kingdom of God, Jesus more often speaks of it as a present reality than a future hope. Can it be that my failure to live in the present puts me in danger of missing the peace and joy of the Kingdom?

We will look at other tree species later on. Why not find an Ash and simply spend some time there? Feel the bark; gently explore the flexible green twigs with their characteristic black buds. Let the slim, graceful leaves slip through your fingers and ask for the grace of feeling the life that is within the tree and you that flows between you and this creature and holds both in love.

If you find an Ash tree that has died you may spot a round black, golf-ball sized fungus. This is not Ash Dieback but a rather useful creature called King Alfred's Cake. Collect some; leave the rest to continue the valuable work of decay and rebirth, and dry it at home (leaving it in a dry place is usually good enough but a warm windowsill will speed up the process). Once dried it acts as a very good firelighter and will have a far smaller environmental impact than the paraffin-based product you find in supermarkets. And of course it is free! If you are doing the coppice woodland thing, it is time to think about a wood burning stove for your house too. There is no better firewood than Ash, which ironically burns so well it leaves very little ash.

## Chapter 2

# Red Ant – encountering the 'other'

*the ants are a people without strength,*
*yet they provide their food in the summer*
– Proverbs 30:25 (NRSV)

In writing about other creatures, and especially animals, I am aware of how easy it is to project human qualities onto them rather than to allow them to teach me. Ants are one of a few creatures in these pages where this tendency is particularly acute, so instead of speaking about them in fairly obvious terms (community, industry, humility, determination, strength and so on) I want to dwell on their "other-ness", a theme that informs my reflections on all the creatures in this book, and my relationship with God.

The Red Ants in our garden have built an impressive nest, a network of tunnels right underneath an old tile we laid down specifically for our young children to lift and find wildlife! So they are both mysterious and hidden. Only when we gently lift the tile are they revealed. The nest is feverish with activity (although that is in large part prompted by us disturbing them) but what tasks are being performed is hard to see. In one sense we know quite a lot about these amazing creatures, but can we even begin to imagine the world from their perspective? And are they so connected that they share a common mind, as is sometimes supposed? We may find it easier to imagine the world viewed from God's perspective than from the Ants' (although thinking we know anything of God's experience exposes our lack of humility more than anything else). It was the theologian Karl Barth who famously said "Let God be God", one of those neat sayings that contains so much.

It is telling that an internet search "what can we do for red ants?" yields a lot of advice about how to mitigate their bite, and even more about how to destroy them. I will highlight and applaud the notable exception, an American (Texas) website called "Beneficials in the Garden". Although the author focuses on a different species (Red Imported Fire Ants), much of what she says is also true of our common Red Ant. I love the honesty with which she owns her prejudices and the effort she has made to present a balanced view. The best thing we can do for this common species, as with others, is to be respectful, learn what we can and, as much as possible, leave them alone.

## From Exodus 3:2-3, 5-6 (NRSV)

*... the angel of the Lord appeared to [Moses] in a flame of fire out of a bush; he looked, and the bush was blazing, yet it was not consumed. Then Moses said, "I must turn aside and look at this great sight, and see why the bush is not burned up." ... Then [God] said, "Come no closer! Remove the sandals from your feet, for the place on which you are standing is holy ground." He said further, "I am the God of your father, the God of Abraham, the God of Isaac, and the God of Jacob." And Moses hid his face, for he was afraid to look at God.*

## For reflection and prayer

The "theophany" (encounter with God) described in Exodus 3 contains a number of elements: Moses is drawn towards the bush but also warned to keep his distance; the bush burns but is not consumed; the bush is "over there" and holy, but the ground upon which Moses is standing is also holy (and by removing his sandals a barrier between the man and the earth is set aside); God is indeed 'other' but speaks in a voice Moses can hear and understand; God calls himself the God not of Moses himself but of his ancestors; and the name of God, at once revealing but also mysterious, is revealed for the first time.

Choose one of these tensions listed above and take some time to consider it, speaking to God as you feel prompted, and making notes in your journal. If you can observe ants of any species then take some time to do so, asking God for the grace to let go of what you expect to see. You may wish to ask also for the grace of releasing your grip on what you think you know of God. The journey is one of stripping away what is not essential, returning to the core, or source. Take some time to be still and speak the word "you" to God. Realise you are also being regarded and responded to. God speaks this word "you" also. Be strangers, then, to one another that a true encounter may emerge.

## Chapter 3

# Badger – digging deeper

In common with most of our native mammals, the Badger is shy and therefore hard to observe. He is very orderly, keeping setts fastidiously clean, and regularly replacing old bedding (bluebells are a favourite material). His staple diet is earthworms but he is an opportunistic omnivore, enabling him to thrive even when for various reasons worms are in short supply. He does have a capacity for extreme aggression, which has led to "baiting" with dogs (where the phrase "to badger" someone comes from), a practice which has been illegal since 1835.[8] Badgers killed this way are sometimes left by roadsides as if killed by cars, although many die on the roads too. In fact the violence of the Badger is overstated – it only surfaces when he is cornered. Like most mammals he acts on the basis that discretion is the better part of valour.

> The Badger trotted forward a pace or two; then grunted, 'H'm! Company,' and turned his back and disappeared from view. 'That's JUST the sort of fellow he is!' observed the disappointed Rat. 'Simply hates Society!
> – Kenneth Grahame, *The Wind in the Willows*

In fact the solitary badger is a total fiction.[9] He spends his entire life with others in social groups. A colony will have a well-established territory (usually about two and half square kilometres or one square mile), comprising between three and six setts, with a 'main sett' (covering around sixty square metres) near the centre. In the winter the group will usually retreat to this, in much the same way as the ancient Norse and Saxon people would have gathered in their 'great halls'.

Setts have been described as "one of the most long-lasting and complex underground burrowing systems on earth". They are passed on from generation to generation, so some are centuries old, but every Badger has an innate urge to dig, even if the sett is already enormous! Tunnels can extend for hundreds of metres and have a number of exits at different heights. This keeps them well ventilated, and allows the occupants to appear and disappear in different places, giving them a well-earned reputation for illusion.

Badger reminds us that there is a place in life for reticence, even secrecy (more about this in chapter 30). He demonstrates positive use of great strength/energy, able to shift great quantities of earth but reluctant to be aggressive towards others. His strong jaw is linked by some to the power of words, and especially storytelling, and his tough skin suggests an ability to receive criticism without becoming hard-hearted. Do you know anyone who cannot receive praise but seems to absorb criticism like a sponge? This is really a false humility, avoiding change rather than enabling it.

It is a simple fact that not everyone can be trusted, but over time trust can be developed. Beware those who expect trust to come in a day! And yet so many courses and training events, in a misguided attempt to minimise cost, attempt to sidestep the essential business of simply being together and building real relationship.[10] Churches, similarly, seem to think you can appoint spiritual leaders through a process of competitive interviewing, despite the fact that these roles depend upon relationship, and knowing, far more than the ability to impress interviewers.

Spending around seventy per cent of his time underground, Badger is more closely connected to earth than some of the other mammals mentioned in these pages. This reminds us that there are times when we need to go back to what is familiar, reconnecting with family or an old friend, or to a place where we have known peace. It may mean paying particular attention to the stories that shaped your early life, and those you have told about yourself. God loves our story and weaves it into a new one, so this action of going back to our roots is not regressive so much as healing. Badger encourages us to build healthy communities rather than retreat into the "nuclear family" that has dominated the last few generations, and find solutions in relationship rather than through disembodied systems. So he calls us back to the heart of Christian faith which is not a set of rules but a living relationship with God. The "Pure Spirit" website[11] sums up beautifully the Badger-like qualities we can embody: "Dig deeper, tell stories, make alliances".

What can we do for Badgers? Drive more slowly, especially in the countryside, and actively reduce car use. Because their setts develop over long periods a more long-term outlook is needed for land where they are in residence, and we need to think bigger about the land as a whole, rather than breaking it into units that do not relate to each other.[12] Their natural predators – wolves and bears – were taken out of the picture centuries ago. It may seem perverse, but predator/prey relationships are important, and rewilding[13] programmes could be very good for badgers as a whole. We also need to challenge the tendency for human beings to persecute them unnecessarily.[14] [15]

## From Deuteronomy 6:5-7 (NRSV)

*You shall love the Lord your God with all your heart, and with all your soul, and with all your might. Keep these words that I am commanding you today in your heart. Recite them to your children and talk about them when you are at home and when you are away, when you lie down and when you rise.*

## For reflection and prayer

This strong and unwavering command resonates like the voice of a conservative preacher holding forth in an uncompromising chapel. It can be hard to take, even from God. But the preacher and his chapel came a long time after these words were first said, and his context was vastly different. How can we escape from that and allow them to speak without filters and qualification? These teachings remind us that we are made up of stories, and that our story is valuable and valued. The encouragement to *remember* is the reason why such a rich storytelling tradition survives amongst Jews and Christians. It is why so many ancient texts have survived, giving us unparalleled insight into the human story as it has unfolded over millennia.

Can we be commanded to love? Again, this can at first seem controlling and egotistical. And yet we are surely at our most alive, our most beautiful, when we love. We speak about "enthusiasm", literally en-*theos*-iasm, when we see a person's face light up with joy as they speak about something or someone they love.

Where are the roots of your life, and what stories have you been told about yourself that have become internalised? And what about God? How do you respond when you are told to love God with your whole being? Can you talk to God about that?

Set out on a prayerful walk and look out for sticks, leaves, fruit, berries, feathers; whatever you can find. Only collect those you feel moved inwardly towards. When you have gathered them set them out prayerfully, allowing the different items to speak to you about parts of your life story. A stone, for example, may stand for an obstacle you once encountered or a heaviness that remains from some past event. A budding stick may represent opportunities you have had or things you wish to give thanks for. You may wish to continue developing this sculpture/montage over the coming weeks, laying them out on the ground or on a white sheet in your home. Think about the pattern they make and try not to impose a pattern too strongly upon them. How do they speak to one another? Which ones are particularly prominent? Which are no longer as significant as they were?

## Chapter 4

# Raven – the incredible reach of God

It can be tempting when you see a large crow to think she is a Raven, but you have to think bigger than you realise. With a wingspan of around 1.2m (4 feet in old money) she is the largest perching bird in Europe, bigger than a Buzzard. She is highly intelligent (as humans rate this)[16] and her life expectancy is comparable to most of ours. More common across Scotland than in the rest of the UK, she favours high ground, often in quite desolate locations; although elsewhere in the world she is more of a forest creature. This may say something about our lack of forests, not to mention her adaptability.

As befits such a large creature, her flight is powerful and purposeful and she comes across as confident and curious. She is capable of great agility,[17] although she eats mostly carrion and the hunting she does is on the ground rather than on the wing: small mammals, eggs, chicks and insects. When food is abundant she creates caches in rocky crevices against leaner times that are ahead.

Breeding begins as early as February, when the highlands are still in the grip of winter and the equinox is still over a month away. The pair share the work of building their nest, gathering and weaving together large sticks, moss, grass and anything else that comes to beak and claw, sticking it all together with mud. This will be the home of just one clutch of between three and seven eggs. She incubates these alone for around three weeks, relying entirely upon her mate for food. Once they have fledged, between five and seven weeks after hatching, the young remain dependent upon their parents for about a month but it is not uncommon for family groups to stick together for longer than this. When the following autumn comes those who are still around will disperse of their own accord, moving into adjacent areas. Otherwise she is fairly solitary. She does not migrate, but will make forays away from her breeding area.[18]

Raven holds a well-established place in folklore. Two Ravens – Hugin (thought) and Munin (desire)[19] – accompanied Odin in Norse mythology, and could be seen as a kind of archetype, so do not be surprised if you encounter her in your dreams. The dark messenger probably indicates something that you are not facing up to, especially if you find the image disturbing. A lot of people have a fear of birds, of course, and Raven is probably one of the most intimidating (have a look at Edgar Allen Poe's poem *The Raven* for example), but if you are able to accept your "shadow" she may become a source of great inspiration, playfulness and creativity. Learning not to be afraid of the dark is an important step in our maturing, as it is itself a fear of the unknown, especially our own death. Raven feeds on the dead – in the past this included battlefields of course – and so it is not surprising that folklore ascribes to her the ability to sense where someone has died. Contemplating her may also help with a fear of being alone or a fear of silence, which stem from the same root. As we will see in a moment, God is far more accepting and embracing than we are. There is nothing to fear.

With roughly seven and half thousand breeding pairs here she is not considered endangered, but I have never seen her in the wild. Have you? Research carried out by the RSPB in 2009[20] established that she is not the cause of other birds' decline, despite the claims of those who wanted permission to wipe her out without pausing to reflect. This has always been the problem historically, but thankfully we have robust legislation in this country to prevent – or at least discourage – the ignorant from taking matters into their own hands. There is some evidence at the time of writing that populations are spreading eastwards, so find out where they are now and whether you might be favoured by some new neighbours.

## From 1 Kings 17:2-4 (NRSV)

*The word of the Lord came to [Elijah], saying, "Go from here and turn eastward, and hide yourself by the Wadi Cherith, which is east of the Jordan. You shall drink from the wadi, and I have commanded the ravens to feed you there."*

## For reflection and prayer

The provision of food by Ravens may hark back to the one who first flew from the ark in search of land (Genesis 8:7). That individual never returned to the ark but continued to search until the land began to reappear. It was the Dove who first returned empty-beaked and then later with the iconic olive leaf. Apart from this Ravens do not feature very heavily in scripture, but there are a couple of places where they are singled out:

*Who provides for the raven her prey, when her young ones cry to God, and wander about for lack of food?*
– Job 38:41 (NRSV)

*He gives to the animals their food, and to the young ravens when they cry.*
– Psalm 147:9 (NRSV)

Interestingly in both of these quotations it is God providing for the Ravens, and specifically their young, rather than Ravens providing for anyone else. The Hebrew word here is *oreb*, which may be a more generic term like Corvid.[21] But of particular interest here is this verse:

*These you shall regard as detestable among the birds. They shall not be eaten; they are an abomination: the eagle, the vulture, the osprey... every raven of any kind*
– Leviticus 11:13, 15 (NRSV)

So what is being said here by the presence of an "unclean" bird that brings food? Presumably God could have chosen any creature to be the bearer of sustenance to Elijah. Just two chapters on (1 Kings 19:5-8) he sends angels. So why choose the Raven?

One of the great revelations that unfolds throughout the Bible is that God's intention has always been to redeem the whole earth. God's people had always been called to be a light to the Gentiles (non-Hebrews), not just their own tribes. The praise offered to God came from all living things (Psalm 150:6), not just humans, and the early disciples were well aware that God's plan was for all creation not just a few people (Psalm 98:3, Jeremiah 23:24, Mark 16:15, James 1:18). Here in Elijah's experience we see the "unclean", the "outsider" becoming not just added to the plot but integral to it. God is pleased to provide for all creatures, not just those who are "kosher", and includes them in the story of the world's salvation. Elijah is provided for by a "Gentile" bird and then, in an even more surprising development, is sent by God to a town in the land of the queen who is seeking to have him assassinated. It is there that he will be hidden, again by an outsider (not just a non-Hebrew but also a widow, someone who traditionally would have relied on others for support and therefore hardly able to feed and shelter someone else), until the time of judgment comes to an end.

The point is pretty clear: God uses the most unlikely ways and people to provide help to those who are called. The strong, the powerful, the beautiful, the charismatic, the accomplished, the qualified – these cannot glorify God. If you do not believe me, look at how God dismisses the greater part of an army (Judges 7:2-7), whittling it down from thirty-two thousand to just three hundred before sending them against a superior force. We can draw a few other important conclusions as well: there is no place in God's scheme for racism, sexism, ageism or elitism of any kind. That is why the Church of England, quite rightly, has made it a disciplinary matter for any of its clergy who belong to political groups that promote this kind of hate.[22]

The Raven has always been a dark figure in human imaginations. This story about Elijah, whose whole life prefigured the coming of Jesus, shows us that no one and nothing is beyond the reach of God's compassion and calling.

# Chapter 5

# St George's Mushroom – the life within

Foraging has no specific season. There are always things to collect whatever the time of year, but the coming of spring brings a clear change in what you gather. Cranberries give way to Elderflowers, Cowberries to Sorrel, and Guelder Rose to Dandelion and Stinging Nettles (yes, we all called them "weeds" once!) Arguably the "Holy Grail" of foraging for wild food is mushrooms. Some of them are incredibly good and, if bought from retailers, incredibly expensive, so the allure is plain. The only fly (agaric?) in the ointment is the danger of death, or horrible sickness. It takes an experienced mycophile to be able to confidently gather these humble creatures for the pot. Anyone who does so has not only to develop the knowledge and skills needed to identify what can be safely eaten, they also have to overcome the dreadful warnings instilled by anxious parents and well-meaning teachers who, unintentionally, also communicated that nature in general is unsanitary, best avoided and must be washed away as soon as possible to preserve life and limb.

So here you are, walking along a field or woodland edge in late April when you see a number of large, white mushrooms forming part of a circle around the base of a tree. They have thick stems (2-4cm wide) and large (5-15cm across), smooth, creamy white/beige caps. The tree may be Oak, Beech, Hazel or Silver Birch. The soil is probably alkaline, although as a walker you might only know that if you are on chalk downland. You may also have seen some on mown grass near to a hedge. This is almost certainly the St George's Mushroom. If so, he is good to eat, but please be advised that people more expert than me think that two other species – both poisonous – look somewhat like him. I didn't know about either of those before I made my omelette in 2011, however, and I am still here to tell the tale. The two suspects are the encouragingly named Deadly Fibrecap and its more innocuous-sounding but also dangerous cousin the White Fibrecap. In fact the differences are clear. You just need to familiarise yourself with them. Read up on all three and you should be able to eat the right one. But this is not a book about foraging. The point is that he is the first mushroom to appear out of the winter chill, so the biggest clue is that it is early spring, as almost every other mushroom appears later on and most only in the damp days of autumn.

The fairy-ring plays a significant role in folklore, of course, marking places where small but powerful spirits were said to gather. Beyond that I have to confess my online searches overwhelmed me with a mishmash of ideas and assertions, very few of which seemed to be grounded in any kind of fact. One website argued, for example, that St Nicolas was a tribal shaman who used mushrooms to get high and that this is what the whole Christmas season is really about!

Fungi in general are hard to classify. Some scientists place them in a separate kingdom from those of animals and plants. St George's Mushroom, like so many mushrooms, is inextricably linked to decay. Turning the rotting leaf litter into new flesh, he represents letting go, rebirth and hope. Ageing and death are not welcome in modern "developed" societies and yet they are a part of life's natural procession. Although we are now in the springtime, this mushroom points us towards autumn, that time of year when we are most strongly reminded, if we have the eyes to see it, that ageing is beautiful.[23] We are not meant to live forever, at least not in the sense that we understand; to do so would be to deny future generations their turn. It is our task in older adulthood to hand over to the next generation and to allow ourselves to be served and, finally, to relinquish our hold on all that we have known and entrust ourselves to the future. Sadly, we do not have many ways of embodying these realities today, and ageing is seen as loss and failure. The elderly worry about being a burden, and the chief focus is often on the cost of care. This is because we have lost the natural life of the extended family within the village setting. That in itself would not be so bad if we had replaced it with something else, but we have not. Professor Nicholas Money[24] presents very succinctly – perhaps too succinctly – the role that fungi in general, and mushrooms in particular, play in the complex system we know as planet earth. He states, having studied them for 30 years, that terrestrial life, and particularly human life, would be impossible without them. The function they play in the environment is essential; the natural mechanisms they use are truly breathtaking:

> Once exposed, the gills of a meadow mushroom shed an astonishing 30,000 spores per second, delivering billions of allergenic particles into the air every day.... some species are capable of spawning the largest and longest-lived organisms on the planet

Interestingly he also believes that they disprove the existence of God. This is quite a claim. In fact what he demonstrates is that, under the influence of certain mushrooms, human beings can have unusual experiences. So we are back to the real meaning of Christmas. Perhaps all we can confidently say is that mushrooms are definitely used by all sorts of people for their own purposes. So one of the messages of this creature to us may be that we need to look beyond our own agenda and be still before very real, earthy things that we do not fully comprehend. Life is truly full of wonder, even after dissection and description have left little to look at. As well as being some of the longest-lived creatures on the planet, there are mushrooms (technically only the fruiting body of the fungus) that appear for only a single day. St George's Mushroom is around a little longer than that, traditionally appearing around 23rd April (St George's Day), hence the name. When we look upon him we need to remember that we see only what is on the surface. What we pick does not capture the whole creature. When we use him for our own purpose we are not realising his full potential, or ours. That does not lie within our gift.

One final warning before you get the oil in the frying pan: cut him open first. There are creatures other than you that have a taste for this species and if they are in there it might make you think twice!

What can we do for Mushrooms? Well, they are pretty robust. Even picking every single one you find will not destroy them (although this would be a pretty selfish and destructive, not to say pointless, action). But if you want to see mushrooms in your garden try letting some of the lawn grow uncut until the end of the autumn. This will have a number of positive benefits, as it will provide a habitat for beneficial insects, which in turn attracts birds, and it gives your lawn a chance to reseed itself. You may be surprised to discover the many grass species that exist in your lawn, as the seed heads give away the differences. It also allows wild flowers to spring up. But in the autumn when the rain comes and everything becomes damp and mushy, the fungi in your lawn will appear at the edge of this long grass. The more different types you see the healthier your garden is.

### From 1 Kings 2:1-3, 5-6, 8-9 (NRSV)

*When David's time to die drew near, he charged his son Solomon, saying: "I am about to go the way of all the earth. Be strong, be courageous, and keep the charge of the Lord your God, walking in his ways and keeping his statutes, his commandments, his ordinances, and his testimonies, as it is written in the law of Moses, so that you may prosper in all that you do and wherever you turn...*

*"Moreover you know also what Joab son of Zeruiah did to me,*

*how he dealt with the two commanders of the armies of Israel, Abner son of Ner, and Amasa son of Jether, whom he murdered, retaliating in time of peace for blood that had been shed in war, and putting the blood of war on the belt around his waist, and on the sandals on his feet. Act therefore according to your wisdom, but do not let his gray head go down to Sheol in peace.... There is also with you Shimei son of Gera, the Benjaminite from Bahurim, who cursed me with a terrible curse on the day when I went to Mahanaim; but when he came down to meet me at the Jordan, I swore to him by the Lord, 'I will not put you to death with the sword.' Therefore do not hold him guiltless, for you are a wise man; you will know what you ought to do to him, and you must bring his gray head down with blood to Sheol."*

## Reflection, prayer and exercise

This Bible reading, like the St George's Mushroom, reminds us that there is often more to things than meet the eye. After all, here is David, the great servant of God, ordering two assassinations from his death bed, including one against someone he had publicly forgiven! But God knows what is in our hearts.

Perhaps there are other senses we can use to approach not only nature but also the situations we find ourselves in. I once worked with a very gifted man who gave me a simple set of questions that help unpack what might be happening in an encounter with someone beyond the words, things that helped get at deeper truths: What are they like to be with? What did you feel during the situation? Perhaps this is what they were, or are, feeling about you or themselves. Or perhaps this is what they want to "put into" you. Some people invade us and even threaten to consume us. Our tendency is to resist, to try to shake off the feeling, but that also includes denying that some part of them has got into us. The very day I completed this chapter I had recalled a woman who was very unpleasant to me. She was terminally ill at the time and is almost certainly no longer alive, and yet to/in me she seems to go on living, her words still exerting an effect. We can easily forget that the authors of the Bible acknowledge the more unpleasant aspects of human relating, and that God is aware of all of it.

When you read this is there anyone who springs immediately to mind? Perhaps a word here and now with that person, who is still with you, is needed. Say what you need to say but do not allow them to speak, only to listen. Then turn and speak to God about them and take your leave. Leave that person with God. If they follow you then do the same again. Do not let them speak, but tell God yourself what they said and what it meant to you. Then walk away again. You may find it helpful to recite Psalm 118 as a closing prayer.

# Chapter 6

# Rook – prophecy, protection and the sharing of wisdom

Rooks and humans have something of a special relationship because when these islands were thickly wooded we were the ones who rapidly increased the number and size of clearings.[25] We then compounded the benefit to Rooks by routinely turning over soil, making worms in particular, but other creatures too, far more readily available. Mature trees at the edges of the villages, farmsteads and fields we established provided the perfect nesting site for these birds that adapted – possibly at the same time, possibly before – to live in large colonies and seek for food in open areas. Rookeries can become very large indeed given the right conditions, with up to ten thousand individuals, and one was found to comprise nearly seven thousand nests, suggesting twice as many breeding pairs. Prior to the devastating disease that all but erased it from the countryside, the Elm was always their favourite nesting tree. Now they are found in many different types of tree, although Oaks (see separate chapter) appear to be the most favoured.

There is a myth that she eats grain and so she is sometimes seen as a pest. In fact where this occurs it is a problem of our own making. She will attack crops, but only if her normal food is in short supply. Her preference is worms, caterpillars, Leatherjackets (Crane Fly Larvae)and other insects, including some that themselves attack crops. She belongs to the Corvid family of birds (the more common term "crows" is confusing because it includes the species that is generally called Crow). There are over one hundred and twenty Corvid species of which the genus Corvus, which includes Rooks, makes up a third.

The blackness of Rook's plumage lends her a sinister look,

especially in the early grey mist of late winter. For this reason she is often linked to death. It was once believed that a Rook perching on a house meant that one of its inhabitants would soon die. But like death, which Tolkein[26] referred to as "the gift of man" [sic], the fear she – or more accurately they, as she is almost never alone – attract is unfounded. Those familiar with the Tarot[27] will know that death is the gateway to new life and is therefore not automatically a negative card to draw. But I believe the Rook has other lessons to share with us. She seems to have a similar ability to us to recognise patterns and carry "archetypes" in her unconscious. Seeing a straight rod or stick in a walker's hand, for example, will prompt an alarm call – she has learned the hard way to be wary of guns. She and others with her will stand sentinel for the whole colony and the alarm will cause the whole group to take flight in an instant. So the Rook may be seen as a prophetic figure, warning us to be sensitive to what is around us and reminding us that we are all part of the greater whole, like a body with many parts. She is also, as we have seen, the victim of a great injustice: it is our doing that her colony is so large, but like many a true prophet she is the one made to pay for it.

An online search for "are rooks protected?" yielded a flood of hits about how to "control" (i.e. kill) them, although I was pleased to find a forum thread in which someone complaining about the rookery in her "beautiful woodland" got short shrift as nine respondents pointed out how fortunate she was to live in such a place. It bears out the point above: we have simply lost touch of any sense that we share this world with others and that that is actually good for us. In fact, like all wild birds in the UK, Rooks are protected.[28] There are some interesting threads online in which people talk quite openly about breaking this law, but thankfully none of them are particularly recent at the time of writing. Encouraging healthy insect populations is one of the best ways to help these birds, although they are not particularly in danger, but switching to organic methods of farming and land management will improve biodiversity in general, bringing back rarer species and helping to nurture balance.

## From Ezekiel 3:17-19 (NRSV)

*Mortal, I have made you a sentinel for the house of Israel; whenever you hear a word from my mouth, you shall give them warning from me. If I say to the wicked, "You shall surely die," and you give them no warning, or speak to warn the wicked from their wicked way, in order to save their life, those wicked persons shall die for their iniquity; but their blood I will require at your hand. But if you warn the wicked, and they do not turn from their wickedness, or from their wicked way, they shall die for their iniquity; but you will have saved your life.*

## For reflection and prayer

The cry of the first murderer was "Am I my brother's keeper?" (Genesis 4:9) to which the short answer was simply yes! Throughout the Bible we see emerging a vision of a people who are called to be the keepers of all humanity (Isaiah 49:6, Luke 2:32), and so in our own time one of the hallmarks of a healthy church is that it is engaged in promoting environmental awareness, justice and peace, serving not only its own interests but those of the world (Isaiah 58:6). Like the Rooks, it is often the squabbles that we are most aware of, and they seem sometimes to be endless. But if we are able to step back can we not also see the signs of the Kingdom about which Jesus spoke? Arguments most often arise among those with whom we live most closely. But when Jesus said "Love your enemies" (Matthew 5:44) he wasn't talking about those we find difficult but those who damage us, and may even wish us dead. Who is in your life and community that seems to wear you down? Can you name them before God, asking for them to receive a special grace, healing and a new way forward?

The role of the prophet – one that the community of Jesus shares, not just a burden for individuals to bear – is rarely an easy one. In our own day the warnings about Climate Change seem to fall on mostly deaf ears. There are even people who want to question the science and suggest it is all still a matter of debate. Our responsibility is not merely to point to the dangers, something that does not seem to be particularly effective (after all, environmentalists have been warning about Climate Change for over thirty years) but to invite people to a new, genuinely beautiful future in which we live in harmony as part of Creation. It seems to me that we can summarise the charism of the Rook as prophecy, protection and the sharing of wisdom. This is what the Church does at its best and where these are lacking in churches we should rightly call into question whether they are really worthy of the name.

# Chapter 7

# Brown Trout – celebrating diversity

*I have heard of a Macedonian way of catching ... fish with speckled skins ... [which] feed upon a fly peculiar to the country, which hovers on the river ... they do not use these flies at all for bait for fish; for if a man's hand touch them, they lose their natural colour, their wings wither, and they become unfit food.... [instead] they fasten red wool around a hook, and fix onto the wool two feathers which grow under a cock's wattles.... and the fish, attracted and maddened by the colour, comes straight at it, thinking from the pretty sight to gain a dainty mouthful....*
– The Roman writer Aelian, AD 170-230

His is the only Trout species native to Britain but they make up for it by being incredibly diverse. Their cells have between thirty-eight and forty-two pairs of chromosomes (compared to humans usual twenty-three). There are freshwater and coastal varieties (the latter are referred to as "sea trout") and as much difference between individuals as we might find in any group of people.

A double row of strong teeth on the roof of his mouth (technically referred to as 'vomerine' teeth) shows him to be a fearsome predator. Although he does not have the usual stereoscopic vision found in many predators, he still has excellent eyesight and uses the polarity of the light to judge distances. His eyes are remarkable structures that enable him to focus on more than one point with the same eye. He can literally see everywhere at once and because, as with most fish, they are on the sides of his head he has an almost complete sphere of visual awareness. His food is usually insects and their larvae, but the largest of his kind have been known to take Voles and other small mammals or young birds that fall into the water. Some will eat other fish, given certain conditions. The abundance of his preferred food seems strongly related to acidity, or rather the lack of it, and this will directly impact his size and rate of growth.

This acute vision, coupled with a good sense of smell, enables females to carefully select their mates, avoiding inbreeding and signs of ill health, both things that bedevil farmed populations (see below).

It has been observed that Trout often occupy the same stretches of river as another native species, the Grayling. They seem to be able to coexist – the website of the Wild Trout Trust (see listed websites in Further Reading) speaks of "habitat niches" – and even though they can share the same prey, there does not seem to be any competition. No one is quite sure how this works, but I would suggest that they have had plenty of time to work out how to coexist (about which more later).

His first scales appear when he is just a month old and they grow by having new layers of hard tissue added each year. This gives away his age, much like the "growth rings" of trees. Most of his kind die in the first year of life, victims of predation or disease, and the longer he lives the better his chances of survival. If he manages to avoid the usual pitfalls he can live to be twenty. His size will be in part determined by population density, especially in lakes. The more there are, the smaller each one will be. He is poikilothermic (the popular phrase is "cold-blooded" but that is misleading. He has the same body temperature as his environment) and can function between 2°C and 25°C. His life, like ours, goes through stages – infant, juvenile, adult, older adult – with a predictable rise and then slow decline of reproductive capability. In so called "developed" societies we do not seem to celebrate this trajectory, or recognise its innate beauty. It has also been observed that, over time, a population of Trout learn to distinguish the lures of people fishing from real prey. This suggests he can probably learn from observation, but it may also be that there is a form of communication that we do not know how to recognise.

Fiercely territorial (somewhat less so in lakes for some reason), he will approach other Trout with strong body language, with both fish gaping their mouths, flaring their gills and darkening their skin tone. Usually the realisation that an opponent is bigger will cause one to back down, actually dropping to the river bed as if dead, with everything closed: mouth, fins, gills – he will even go slightly pale. Fights are rare. There is a paradox here as well, because he will migrate up and down river during his lifetime, so territories may not be as fixed as might be the case with other creatures.

I could, of course, write "work to stop climate change" on every page, but Trout is one creature that is particularly susceptible to its effects. Changing temperatures inevitably affect the most dynamic habitats first and freshwater environments are among these. Temperature has a direct effect on the length of different life stages and a change in temperature fluctuations (the phrase "global warming" suggests a steady, equally distributed rise, but this is not what happens on the ground or in the water) and the temperature of water dictates all manner of other properties too: how much oxygen it can hold, what other species may be able to move in, the balance and behaviour of naturally occurring chemicals, the presence or absence of essential microbes. These are just the most obvious. Perhaps you can think of others.

Other measures include protecting naturally alkaline wetlands from acidification (through pollution or the presence of coniferous trees), ensuring that fields' neighbouring watercourses are not overgrazed (which leads to bank erosion and the consequent silting up of river beds), limiting angling (which removes larger, fertile fish from populations), prevention of barriers to migration, reducing the populations of domesticated fish (which seem to have poorer immune systems due to greater inbreeding) and keeping them away from wild populations, and making sure that human interventions do not change the established seasonal variation in flow of any given river (which has been demonstrated to be directly linked to the success or failure of Trout to reproduce).

## From Job 12:7-10 (NRSV)

*...ask the animals, and they will teach you;*
*the birds of the air, and they will tell you;*
*ask the plants of the earth, and they will teach you;*
*and the fish of the sea will declare to you.*
*Who among all these does not know*
*that the hand of the Lord has done this?*
*In his hand is the life of every living thing*
*and the breath of every human being....*

## For reflection and prayer

One of the realities of writing a book like this is that I am not only working with what is known, but also with the way facts are commonly presented. On every page I am talking about a fictitious individual who might be seen as typical of her or his species. The problem with this, as Wendell Berry points out in his superb essay *Life is a Miracle* (see Further Reading), is that there is no such thing as a "typical" anything. We are all individuals and this applies to a Trout as much as to a human being. Each one of us is used to thinking of ourself as a person with a name and a story, relationships and experiences, unique fingerprints, a rich inner life. How often do we apply this to other creatures? It is not easy. They do not use names as we do. Many of them do not have a language we can recognise, much less understand. None of us is comfortable with the thought that our life might really be boiled down to a few facts typical of anyone. If you disagree with this try planning an impersonal funeral for someone and see what happens!

The Brown Trout is potentially more diverse than we are. You might say there are a variety of dialects, faces, bodies and skin colour. It has taken many centuries, even millennia, to accept the variety of humanity. Many, sadly, have not even arrived at that yet. If we are to develop an accurate, humble understanding of ourselves and our part in the great story of life, perhaps the acceptance of the differences within species is one important step. Elsewhere I have taken on the lazy use of relational language, specifically the word "cousin", so often applied across species. My cousins are also human beings. To talk about the Brown Trout and the Rainbow Trout as genetic cousins is an abuse of language and denigrates both species. We have to work harder than this.

The book of Job – the oldest book in the Bible and one of the oldest in the world – makes a fascinating point. It follows the (possibly fictitious) experience of a man who suffers great loss, seemingly without doing anything wrong. The message of the book, which is written in a poetic style and follows the conversation he has with three others about what has happened, seems to be first that undeserved suffering is a reality, second that although God does not cause suffering God does take responsibility for it, and third that the future well-being of Creation will come about through the personal trial of one who suffers. This person, who enters the suffering of the world and becomes one with it, will through that act of suffering bring about a new unity with God and a beautiful, healthful future.

# Chapter 8

# Magpie – peace and trust in the face of uncertainty

She is, of course, another Corvid and her emergence makes me wonder: why is this family of birds coming to prominence as I write? They fly darkly into the imagination, enigmatic and self-contained. So perhaps that question will remain unanswered. Perhaps it is the least valuable of all questions. 'Why?' is something we learn to grasp at a very young age, usually between two and three, when we have begun to develop language but not yet reasoned thought. A battle of wills begins and we are called, invited, to let it go. It is a question firmly located in the past: How did this situation come about? When did it start? Who is responsible? What is the story behind this experience? It is often prompted by pain, discomfort or dissatisfaction. But the answer may not comfort us. The answer may itself be a question that does not need an answer but must be lived with. Eventually, whether we receive an answer or not, we have to live in the present moment. This is one of the mysteries of maturity. We realise that answers are unsatisfying, that life is not a question, or series of questions. Life is not a problem to be solved. It is what it is.

Letting go of something that seems important to us may be the message of Magpie. Her striking black and white colouring is deceptive: up close and at certain angles a metallic bluish hue can be detected. Like us she is fairly omnivorous and can be seen systematically hunting for eggs and young chicks, striking fear into the hearts of parent birds of other, smaller species. Seeing this behaviour it is easy to rush to judgment. We need to remember that the natural world, from which we have foolishly attempted to remove ourselves, maintains its own balance. This is not merely inevitable but good. It keeps populations healthy and embodies the interdependence of all things. In the same way, no matter how hard we pray, God does not protect us from calamity (one of the hardest lessons from the book of Job). This is difficult to grasp, as we want to believe in the loving God of our childhood, but as we grow to adulthood we are invited to develop an adult faith, to pass through the desert of doubt and isolation and discover that there are many things we cannot explain. This is a normal, healthy spiritual journey and not the failure that so many churches seem to treat it as. Beware those who offer you certainty!

There is a myth that Magpie collects shiny objects and is something of a sneak-thief. Since research[29] shows this is not the case, I wonder where it arises, and why certain websites seek to perpetuate it. Perhaps it is the doom of the Corvidae that they will always be subject to unfair projections. With her natural adaptability (she can be found in a variety of habitats right across the UK, the only exception being the highlands of Scotland, she alters her diet throughout the year and in times of plenty stores food in caches against leaner times ahead). Magpie invites us to grow to maturity, recognising the flaws in arguments, how beliefs are stories that exist within their own frames of reference. This does not make them untrue, but we are invited to a humble and perhaps more cautious analysis of the things and people we encounter. Black and white? Not when we draw near.

Concerns about the effect of population increase on other birds (it coincided with a decrease in songbird populations) led the RSPB to carry out research[30] to see if there was any link. In fact they found that it is modern farming practices rather than predation that is the problem and state on their website: "It confirms that populations of prey species are not determined by the numbers of their predators".

Like all the Corvids, Magpie has a piercing gaze. She seems to be able to look beyond the surface, past our pretence, and is quick to beat a retreat from us. This again reminds us to look carefully, to accept the complexity of life and to realise that although we may think of ourselves as benign, we do not always appear that way to others.

We have to refrain from killing them illegally, but that is more for our sake than theirs, since it is hard to prove any just cause to do so. There are legal conditions for proper 'control' (a nice euphemism!) although it is questionable whether any killing is really necessary. As always these laws are for human convenience and utility rather than any sense of the natural balance.

## From Numbers 24:3-4, 17 (NRSV)

*...The oracle of Balaam son of Beor,*
*the oracle of the man whose eye is clear,*
*the oracle of one who hears the words of God,*
*who sees the vision of the Almighty,*
*who falls down, but with eyes uncovered...*
*...a star shall come out of Jacob,*
*and a scepter shall rise out of Israel...*

## For reflection and prayer

What do we think we know? What do we think we see or discern? Most of us learn to trust our instincts, but it is possible to find out that you are wrong. This can be very hard to take. I remember a period in my own life when I began to question any ability I had to make any judgements at all – I just seemed to come up against other people's different views all the time. I did not find an answer for this, and it may be that my judgement is faulty. But in fact there is no objectivity and those who claim to have it are trying to deceive you. So often differences of opinion are resolved not by who is right or wrong but by who holds power. This calls for wisdom, but there will be times in life when we have to move on and never know what the right thing would have been. When confronted with real uncertainty, can I develop the trust that leads to genuine peace? Which comes first: peace or trust?

Find a place outside to be still and fix your gaze on a distant spot. It may be a single leaf a hundred metres or more away, or similar. It doesn't matter what you choose as long as it is small and relatively distant. Remain fixed upon it, attempting to "zoom in" with your vision alone. What ought to happen after only about twenty seconds is that your peripheral vision will blur and may even fade, casting a sort of tunnel effect. Stop if you feel ill! If you find it strains your eyes you are probably tired, so it is best to do this when you are in a good state. If it makes you feel unwell it is because most of us don't do this very often. It is not an endurance test, but an experience. Recognise that having a clear view of one thing can blur your vision of what else is around. Even the most perceptive people can be wrong sometimes.

# Chapter 9

# Peregrine – life in all its fulness

*I saw a crow, quite a large bird, seemingly on her way from one place to another in not much of a hurry, when suddenly she realised this small, dark spot on the edge of vision was getting larger, shooting towards her with astonishing speed. With a terrified squawk, she hurled itself into the nearest tree, crashing into the foliage without any thought except getting away. It was absolutely gripping.*

This observation by a close friend of mine[31] from his back garden demonstrates what a fearsome predator the Peregrine is. Combining speed and agility, he targets a variety of medium-sized birds and easily outmanoeuvres those of a similar size or larger, including our friend the Crow. His preferred style is to take prey in the air, with a plunge of up to 180 Km/h, which would be literally breathtaking if it were not for a special adaptation to his nostrils. It is not unknown for him to catch land animals such as mice, frogs, or lizards but for these he cannot make use of the headlong dive, so if you see this behaviour it probably indicates a lack of food generally. Pigeons appear to be favourite, for rather obvious reasons – a clumsier wild bird native to Britain is hard to imagine – but he will attack almost anything that flies, even something as large as a Heron. This hunting style is fairly chancy: he quite often misses, and no doubt small birds in general know how to jink at the last second to avoid disaster as best they can. It also explains why so many native birds stay close to very solid obstacles like trees and the ground!

Peregrines can be seen all year round in the UK, although they do move about so the ones you see in summer will be different from those you might spot in winter (unless you move with them, of course). Our friend here is male so less likely than his female counterparts to leave the exposed uplands when the days grow shorter and colder. Wales, Scotland and the North of England are the best areas, with decreasing population density as you head south and east. During the summer breeding season he is to be found in the mountains and hills, especially around the coasts of Britain, although the terrain is not as important to him as the availability of prey. In winter the comparatively sheltered marshes of the east coast appear to be favoured. This moving is not proper migration, and the majority of his kind never go much more than a hundred kilometres from their place of birth. Wherever he goes he quickly establishes his boundaries, keeping well clear of others' territories. The size of these is a function of the abundance or otherwise of prey. Scraping out her eyrie (nest) in the most exposed, inaccessible places (she does not build like other birds but simply creates a shallow depression with what is already there), his mate will lay up to four eggs over the course of a week around the beginning of April. The pair will take turns to incubate these for about a month, after which they hatch. There is little difference in size between the oldest and the youngest, but during the following fortnight it is he who will do most of the hunting. Five or six weeks on from hatching the young begin to fledge, and then the process of learning how to hunt and manage prey begins. If they survive – and over two thirds of them will not – they will be fending for themselves within three months. But from here on their chances improve, with the survivors living for five or six years on average.

We should support the rigorous policing of his protected status, which is the highest afforded by UK legislation. It is not only an offence to kill or injure the birds or their nest, but even disturbing them during the breeding season carries a heavy fine and possibly a prison sentence. Too many landowners and their staff poison, trap and shoot Peregrines in an attempt to protect commercial interests (grouse keeping in particular), and there is evidence that pigeon fanciers target them as well. Changes in land use, especially the destruction of forests and hedgerows, can also lead to a decline in prey species.

Because they are predators their bodies accumulate any toxins that are present in their territory. This was disastrous for them in the 1950s but thankfully greater awareness and control of pesticides and the like have enabled numbers to increase again. Their beautiful chestnut-brown speckled eggs can also be a temptation for egg collectors. With only fifteen hundred breeding pairs in the UK we cannot afford to be complacent. I would encourage membership of the RSPB, who have in the last few years broadened their scope to include nature more generally than just birds. They do still speak of nature as if it were something we are separate from: "Give nature a home" strikes me as being particularly strange.[32] It is nature that gives us a home. Even locked in a tiny cubby in a Tokyo "capsule hotel" you are still completely dependent upon nature to keep you alive. But the RSPB has more members than all the political parties of Britain put together, and that alone makes it an organisation worth getting involved with. Because about one fifth of the global population of Peregrines breed here, ours is a global responsibility.

### From Job 39:26-30 (NRSV)

*Is it by your wisdom that the hawk soars,*
*and spreads [his] wings toward the south?*
*Is it at your command that the eagle mounts up*
*and makes [his] nest on high?*
*[He] lives on the rock and makes [his] home*
*in the fastness of the rocky crag.*
*From there [he] spies the prey;*
*[his] eyes see it from far away.*

*[His] young ones suck up blood;*
*and where the slain are, there [he] is.*

## For reflection and prayer

The book of Job is as mysterious as it is powerful. At first we see a man who is brought low through no fault of his own. Indeed he is a paragon of virtue. So the book raises a question that remains a source of confusion to this day: the problem of evil and suffering, and especially the suffering of the innocent. Surrounded by three philosophers, Job finds himself defending his position and although he starts off by being devout, he eventually shakes his fist at God. God's response may seem peculiar to us, but it is also instructive: God shows Job the wonders of creation, going into great detail about the lives of creatures that live in all kinds of different habitats, reminding Job that his life is part of a greater whole. Watching the Peregrine in full flight, whether he catches his prey or not, we too can recapture a sense of awe that has become sadly dulled by too much artificiality. We have a beautiful gift, that of imagination, and with it we too can soar high above the land, keen eyes picking out the movements below, nostrils drawing in the clean, cold air, feathers warmed by the sun.

Pick a morning soon and go for a solitary walk, but wear a thick jumper rather than a coat. There is something important about the more porous nature of this kind of garment. Walking with awareness is a form of prayer, but talking about it – and reading about it – is ultimately meaningless. Prayer is a practice, not a theory. It is something you have to *do*. The power of the Peregrine is that, as he plunges towards his prey, he is fully and sharply alive, and this is what prayer ultimately is all about. So if you haven't time now, make time later. Put it in your diary and go. And, if you can, go somewhere where the Peregrine calls your name.

# Chapter 10

# Water Vole – focussing on what is essential

It was only whilst researching this book that I discovered that we have three different species of Vole: Water Vole, Field Vole and Bank Vole. The first of these will be my focus, and is, in fact, the most rare. This poor lass is the one most commonly mistaken for a Rat because both species tend to live near water courses. Kenneth Grahame's "Ratty" in *The Wind in the Willows* is actually a Water Vole. It is a bit of a shame that this otherwise beautiful work of fiction has given rise to such popular misunderstandings. An employee of Severn Trent Water told me that Rats do not actually like getting wet, so if you see a swimming Rat you are almost certainly looking at a Vole and if you are still confused check the tail: the Water Vole's is furry and only half the length of her body. This confusion is a shame because all Vole species are general herbivores and quite benign, but concern about Rats does lead to a great deal of collateral damage. In fact Rats of all species are foreign to Britain and that is the last I am going to say about them in these pages.

The Water Vole seeks a quiet life, not easy when you are prey for Owl, Stoat, Weasel, Fox and Mink (see below). So alertness and awareness, listening and intuition are embodied here. Discretion too: the entrance to her burrow is often under water and leads to passageways and nest chambers at different levels, presumably to cope with fluctuations in the river. She consumes a huge variety of vegetable matter, as many as 227 different plant varieties according to Government research,[33] but will take invertebrates as well, eating in certain favoured places which can be spotted by the discarded remains of her meals. She may have up to five litters in a year, with as many as seven pups in each. They take four months to reach maturity, although they are weaned at two weeks, so there may be more than one litter in a burrow at a time. Most of these will only breed the following year, and the winter can carry off as many as seventy per cent of them.[34] Generally active in the daytime, she marks her territory (about seventy metres of riverbank – the male territory is larger at a hundred and thirty metres) with "latrines" of faeces. So, a creature with a strong sense of place and of belonging to it; one who moves easily between the different environments of earth (underground), water and land/air; and who is deeply and constantly aware of her mortality.

Her biggest problem by far is predatory Mink,[35] introduced to the UK for his fur around the 1920s and inevitably escaping from farms fairly soon afterwards. The first confirmation of mink populations in the wild was in 1956 and since that time Water Vole populations have crashed.[33] The best thing you can do for them if you do not own land they are on is report their presence to the appropriate Wildlife Trust (see Websites section). If you do own land that may be suitable for them it is not hard to find out what to do.[36] Please let me know if you choose to take on this action – my Twitter account is @MindfulWanderer, or you could contact me via the publisher – I would love to hear about it.

## From Psalm 131 (NRSV)

*O Lord, my heart is not lifted up,*
*my eyes are not raised too high;*
*I do not occupy myself with things*
*too great and too marvellous for me.*
*But I have calmed and quieted my soul,*
*like a weaned child with its mother;*
*my soul is like the weaned child that is with me.*
*O Israel, hope in the Lord*
*from this time on and forevermore.*

## For reflection and prayer

The psalm above is often taken as a model for the monastic calling. Although it suggests a "quiet life", it has to be remembered that it is only one of one hundred and fifty Psalms (a collection of songs for which we no longer have the original music) which together cover a huge range of experiences. So rather than adopting an "either/or" approach, I would suggest a "both/and" one. We can and should be concerned about great matters – it would be irresponsible not to – but there are times when it is important to retreat and recover the sense that we are loved personally and individually. Those who are able to "tirelessly" serve God in various contexts learn this, usually the hard way: a personal prayer life is vital in order to keep going. Like sleep, food and other essentials, we cannot go long without prayer. This is not because God withholds favour from us – we have the assurance that God's love is continually poured out – but because we are free to receive it or not to. This is a mystery that many writers have sought to explore. One of the gifts of a regular prayer life is that it puts you in touch with your finitude, the clear knowledge that you will die one day, and that few of us know exactly when that will be. If this seems negative and morbid, I would suggest that it is the culture we live in, not the facts of life, that needs to change. The knowledge that we will one day die has been described as humanity's gift.[26] Some of the most creative people have been inspired by it[37] and while death is not something to be sought – indeed most healthy creatures will work to avoid it – it has a way of focussing the mind. Whatever we are engaged with, death asks the question "Does this really matter?" And if not, "what would?" So listen to the ever-present watcher and give your life, which means your time, to the things that really count.

## Chapter 11

# Common Frog – rediscovering familiar paths

Leaping suddenly from cover when you least expect him, he can still be hard to spot even when you know he is there. His skin colour varies hugely: green, brown, yellow, orange, black, red or cream. During the mating season he may have a bluish throat, whilst his mate could have a pinkish blush to her skin. His natural camouflage is enhanced by seemingly random dark patches and dark bars on his legs. He needs it, being the prey of foxes, birds of prey, snakes, large predatory fish and domestic cats.

People often wonder if they are seeing a Frog or a Toad, but the leap gives the game away, and the markings of course. There are only two Frog species in Britain, but the nationally extinct Pool Frog was reintroduced in a programme that started in 2005[38] to just one location (Thompson Common in Norfolk), so he may be one of the easiest creatures to positively identify that we have.

He emerges from hibernation in February, depending on conditions, and will make his way to the breeding site – usually a pond – about a month later. This will be the place where he was born. His croaking song attracts a female, somewhat larger than he is, and he grasps hold of her, fertilising her eggs (spawn) when they emerge. Since this only happens when she is ready, he may find himself being lugged about for several days before the moment comes.

Frogspawn forms easily recognisable clumps in the water, each one containing three or four hundred eggs. The tadpoles begin to hatch at one to three weeks. This is a vulnerable time because many pond-dwellers feed on them. Their legs start to appear at between six and nine weeks and after twelve to sixteen weeks (depending on local climate) they start to haul out of the water and go a-roaming. Meanwhile, with breeding completed, our male Frog has long gone, and may have covered quite a distance, perhaps to make room for the young coming up behind him. He catches insects by flicking out his long, sticky tongue and is also something of an opportunist, eating worms, snails and slugs. He does not "breathe" in a biological sense because that definition includes a diaphragm, which he does not have. But he does have lungs, inflating them by using the muscles of his throat, and he also has the strange ability to absorb oxygen through his skin, which is one of the reasons he needs, and thrives in, wet conditions.

It is tempting to poach some spawn (I do not mean two minutes in boiling water!) for your garden pond, but please resist, as you may be helping to spread a disease called Redleg. Create the right conditions and they will come to you (how about a film called *Ponds of Dreams*?) They are widespread throughout the UK and not endangered, and they are quite commonly seen in gardens. But populations have declined in some areas. It is the same old story of habitat loss – we do not use ponds as a resource in the widespread way we used to – and the side-effect of chemical spray which not only hits the wildlife in a field but also drifts into neighbouring areas. Buying organic has an immediate effect on your pocket and you do not immediately see the positive effect on biodiversity, but the more of us who buy into it the healthier everyone and everywhere will be. I firmly believe that it is better to deal with things at source than to solve problems – or to put it in a familiar way, prevention is better than cure. Actually that old saying can be misleading because it suggests that we can cure the ills we cause. We do not apply this to our bodies, do we? Who in their right mind says, "I'll expose myself to serious illness because medicine can fix most problems"? But we say it about the environment. What I am suggesting, then, is that we can do more good by buying organic, seasonal, local produce than by saving our money in the super-market and giving it to environmental charities. I would add that paying a levy of 5p or so for a disposable plastic bag is risible, and giving that 5p to environmental charities is the height of irony. It means that environmentalist fundraisers and activists are relying on plastic bag production for their income when what is needed is a complete ban and the space that creates for normal people like you and me to use our God-given imaginations to come up with better ways to package and transport our goods.

## From Psalm 33:4-6, 20-22 (NRSV)

*...the word of the Lord is upright,*
*and all his work is done in faithfulness.*
*He loves righteousness and justice;*
*the earth is full of the steadfast love of the Lord.*
*By the word of the Lord the heavens were made,*
*and all their host by the breath of his mouth.*
*Our soul waits for the Lord;*
*he is our help and shield.*
*Our heart is glad in him,*
*because we trust in his holy name.*
*Let your steadfast love, O Lord, be upon us,*
*even as we hope in you.*

## For reflection and prayer

He hides and avoids, and this is integral to who he is. It is not a failure of nerve or spirituality to choose anonymity at times, or to hide away. He is moved to find a mate and reproduce. He may be successful, he may not. This too is not failure, it is written into the essence of his soul. He is drawn to return to what he has known by familiar paths, often following scent laid down by himself and others: this is not unimaginative. He roams widely: this is not feckless.

As I was nearing the end of this book's first draft I too felt a need to return to a familiar path. I have tried a number of different prayer styles, but few seem to "stick". This is ok, and failure in prayer is not terminal. For me one of the few practices that have remained over the years is simple Bible reading. So I picked up where I had left off, in the book of Job. The words I found there turned me immediately back to this writing project, a profound affirmation that, at least at the moment, I am on the right track. What will come after is anyone's guess – "the wind blows where it chooses" – and this brings me to something I heard only a year ago, a piece of avowedly secular wisdom[39] that rang true: "You do not have to have a dream". Humans are good at planning, not so good at letting go. This advice may not be right for everyone, but for me there is a joyful freedom in letting go of the long term future, focussing on the *now* and the *soon*. This seems to be what most creatures do, including the Frog. It is the antithesis of our politics, where plans are made and trust is placed in wealth and military power. When Jesus invites us to consider the creatures of the earth, perhaps this is what he means: not to deny our God-given abilities, but to understand them and, in freedom, to choose the present and the soon, trusting that God has a future for us.

## Chapter 12

# Shrew – God's surprising choice

Small, shy and having the ingrained habits of the preyed-upon, it is no wonder I have never seen a Shrew in the wild. Have you? Their life expectancy is incredibly short, even shorter than the Water Vole's or the Kingfisher's, rarely as long as a whole solar year. But they are found all over Britain and some of its islands in a variety of habitats and are, in fact, the second most common native mammal. The Mammal Society website[40] states: "Living at densities of up to 50 per hectare in many woodlands and often over 20 per hectare in grasslands and other habitats, the most recent estimate puts the number of shrews in Britain at 41,700,000".

Shrew's little red teeth sink mainly into insects and she supplements her diet with earthworms, snails and slugs. It does not do for her to be too choosy. Her small size (5-8cm, not including her tail) and high metabolism (in mammals the two often go together) mean she must eat every few hours. This, of course, exposes her to many predators. She secretes an unpleasant-tasting serum from glands on her sides and this puts off most of them. Unfortunately it does not stop domestic cats from killing her. If you find a dead Shrew then this is the most likely cause. Her main natural enemies, though, lurk in the skies above and lack a sense of smell: Tawny and Barn Owls and Kestrels.

Her home is a burrow, probably excavated and left empty by another creature or, because she is an excellent climber, it could be an abandoned nest or even a nest box in a garden. She remains active in the winter months, although she slows down markedly and, amazingly, she actually shrinks a little to improve efficiency. As far as we are aware this is unique among mammals. Unsocial and vigorous in defending her territory, she lets down her guard during the summer breeding season to mate with two or three males. It is not unusual for a single litter (usually around half a dozen pups at a time) to have genetic diversity as a result, and she may have up to four litters during this time. One of the most endearing features of Shrews is the "caravan", in which young form a chain, each holding onto another's tail, to keep up with the mother as she searches for a new nest or forages for food. So despite the name, this not-at-all rare creature gives the lie to the name "common". She is, in fact, utterly remarkable.

She is not even slightly endangered, although along with the other native species, the Pygmy Shrew (yes it *is* possible to be smaller!) and the Water Shrew, she is protected by Schedule 6 of the Wildlife and Countryside Act (1981). Restoring traditional hedgerows and reducing the use of chemical pesticides are two ways landowners can help these fellow countryside-dwellers. If you are fortunate to have a garden that borders woodland or fields you can also create habitat and nesting sites fairly easily and encourage insects by building a "bug hotel" (a simple internet search will show you how, or contact your local Wildlife Trust).

## From Isaiah 53:1-3, 10 (NRSV)

*Who has believed what we have heard? And to whom has the arm of the Lord been revealed? For he grew up before him like a young plant, and like a root out of dry ground; he had no form or majesty that we should look at him, nothing in his appearance that we should desire him. He was despised and rejected by others; a man of suffering and acquainted with infirmity; and as one from whom others hide their faces he was despised, and we held him of no account.*

*...When you make his life an offering for sin, he shall see his*

*offspring, and shall prolong his days; through him the will of the Lord shall prosper.*

## For Reflection and Prayer

The majestic language of Isaiah 53 is undeniably poetic, but with that comes a danger that we miss what is being said. Another translation puts verse 2 like this: "*The servant grew up before God – a scrawny seedling, a scrubby plant in a parched field*" (The Message)[41]. I could put that even more bluntly: like a weed. We all know, do we not, that God chooses the weak and the humble, those who are "of no account" (1 Corinthians 1:27)? We know, do we not, that the power of God is seen in weakness (James 4:6, 2 Corinthians 12:9)? How interesting to see, then, that so many churches continue to have a "hierarchy", "significant positions" and, in at least one Anglican Diocese, the idea of "first-class priests". In the debate about whether women ought to be able to become bishops I have always been broadly in favour, but it has saddened me to see that it is the powerful and the pushy, the educated and erudite, the strong and the sassy, who are being "elevated" (yes, I believe this is the word used) to "senior" roles in the church. Is this because, for all our rhetoric, we still believe in a rather attractive Jesus and we look for "leaders" in this mould? I recall suggesting once that Jesus may have been fat, only to be told that "he wouldn't have eaten too much". I was at theological college at the time. I suggest that this says more about that student's attitude to fat than anything to do with Jesus!

Unattractive, cut off from a long life, distasteful to many, constantly active, even restless, can we accept the Shrew-like qualities of Jesus? Can we let him disappoint us, irritate us, offend us? Can we, in other words, let him be himself? Until we do this, are we not just fashioning an idol with the same name?

# Chapter 13

# Blackbird – the way of the artist

He's bolder than his ancestors were, I am confident of that. Do any digging in your garden or allotment and you are just as likely to see him as that other opportunist, the Robin. He works hard too, systematically working his way through the autumn leaves in search of insects, worms, caterpillars and grubs. We have named his kind after the male, whose black plumage is accentuated by a bright orange/yellow beak and ring encircling each eye. He hops and flits and his song reminds us of the woods that once blanketed these lands. Another solitary creature, he asserts his territory during the autumn while still young. He will energetically defend it through the spring mating and into high summer, but then relaxes when his young have fledged, enjoying a sort of Sabbath over a few weeks before the cycle begins again. During this he will allow other males to cross his borders and he will cross theirs in search of food. So he is both boundaried and adventurous, with a strong sense of season and need. Most creatures are wise in this way, not wasting energy in unnecessary activity, maintaining a sense of what is essential. In contrast we seem to have an amazing ability to focus our attention and energy. The flipside is we can lose perspective and pour ourselves into something that may not be as important as we think, or wish.

He and his mate will expect to raise two or three broods of chicks (three to five at a time) in a normal season. In general the nest is built fairly low down, in what may be called the "middle layer", or "understorey", of forest (a healthy forest will have a canopy, understorey, field and ground layers) and is the classic shape we associate with birds' nests, comprising a cup of woven grass lined with mud, keeping the precious eggs from falling and out of the wind. It is a fine craft, this nest-building, and his mate can take up to a fortnight to complete it, vigorously protecting the site against other females all the while. As he gets older she is likely to be his partner again. He makes himself scarce while she incubates, but returns to help feed the chicks. From hatching to fledging takes just a couple of weeks, although the approach of a predator such as the Magpie can prompt an early departure. This is a time of high mortality, with perhaps up to forty per cent of the eggs/chicks being taken. But if the young are around nine days old or more they have a chance and they will consolidate this by going into hiding on the ground. It is from there that they learn to fly. The juvenile stage is one of experimentation and risk, learning what is food and what is not. During this time they stay within his territory, under his protection, and for most of this time it will be his task to teach them as his mate is already getting ready for the next clutch. He will not drive the young blackbirds away but when they are ready they leave of their own accord, led by an instinct that millions of generations have moulded.

I faced a dilemma only last spring, when a Blackbird chick called for her parents persistently and plaintively on our front lawn. Surely a cat would take her, calling so loudly and obviously and not under cover? But I resisted the urge and spent a stressful evening, with this whistling call appealing to my better nature every twenty seconds. The next morning she was gone and I will never know where. I knew I had done the right thing. It is the way of nature, though it felt harsh and uncaring. But what is the alternative? Could I teach her to feed, to fly and to flee? Our task, as so often, is to leave well alone, and not to impose values that are out of place.

It is the lack of forest that is the issue. It saddens me to see that so many people cut down trees almost as soon as they move into a new place, presumably because they do not want to maintain them. Caring for the trees is one of our tasks as humans, and is itself spiritually fulfilling. We are at our best when we give ourselves to things that will outlive us. We know this is true because we do it for our children.

The Blackbird is not rare – the RSPB estimates up to fifteen million of them spend the winter here[42] – but we need more hedgerows, and not just for Blackbirds. These may be a bit more work but they are alive and far more pleasing than a fence or wall (the exception being stone walls which are themselves home to many kinds of creatures). It is a challenge to let go of our idea of neatness – straight lines, symmetry and conformity – but it takes very little time for a natural order to emerge, and it is in the very idiosyncrasy of living barriers that some of the most beautiful surprises can be found. Although populations are higher in towns, death by starvation there is more common. Planting traditional hedges and native shrubs, which play host to insects and caterpillars, is far better than putting out food because it follows the pattern established over centuries. Traditional hedge-laying, which I am pleased to see is making a comeback, is a nice skill to acquire and a very pleasant winter activity for adults and children alike. There is nothing quite like laying a length of hedge, which gets the body moving, develops attention and thought, and has an immediate outcome you can stand back and admire, ideally with a flask of mulled apple juice or cider and some apple and ginger cake.

### From Ecclesiastes 3:1, 10-13 (NRSV)

*For everything there is a season, and a time for every matter under heaven...*

*I have seen the business that God has given to everyone to be busy with. He has made everything suitable for its time; moreover he has put a sense of past and future into their minds, yet they cannot find out what God has done from the beginning to the end. I know that there is nothing better for them than to be happy and enjoy*

*themselves as long as they live; moreover, it is God's gift that all*
*should eat and drink and take pleasure in all their toil.*

## For reflection and prayer

As a parent, I am constantly enchanted and fascinated by the way
toddlers just "get busy". There seems to be little time wasted in
deciding what they want to do, and no time spent deciding what
they want to achieve. They get stuck in and see what naturally
emerges. This, it seems to me, is the way of the artist, experi-
menting with materials and seeing what emerges naturally. It
seems quite common in art to allow the work to come to birth,
rather than trying to impose order and form. Art emerges from a
relationship between the artist and the material. Science seems to
have begun this way too: curiosity about what was "out there",
and how things work, led to a method of systematic experimentation and observation. This was partly driven by, but also helped
to create, a sense of wonder at the complexity, diversity and
beauty of creation. So both of these traditions have at their heart
a relationship between us and the world we exist within and, at
their best, feed a sense of worship that grows rather than dimin-
ishes as our experience increases.

There seems to be a growing awareness in our time that
physical work is of greater value than we have given it credit for.
For far too long our education system, driven by the desire to
maximize something called "the economy", has more or less
explicitly drawn a line between the intellect and the body, and
placed intellectual work above manual labour. The result is a
wealthy, comfortable, overweight and stressed population. The
idea that a person might be able to have a rich intellectual life *and*
work with their hands seems unusual. But the way children
engage intellectually by getting stuck in is a big clue. I am not
going to focus here on becoming like a child – that is explored in
the chapter on Toad – but rather on this relationship between the
body and the mind. "Lo he abhors not the virgin's womb",

declares one Christmas Carol, in language that conveys a profound truth we can easily lose among the poetry. He does not stop there: he also abhors not the builder's toolbox. It has been suggested that a "carpenter" in Jesus' day was a general builder, who would have had an array of skills, not only carpentry. There may have been some in Galilee who, without realising it, actually had the Lord build their house (see Psalm 127)!

My own life has been transformed in this respect by the author Matthew Crawford, whose book *The Case for Working with Your Hands: or Why Office Work is Bad for Us and Fixing Things Feels Good*, sets all this out far more comprehensively than I have room for here, but here is a snapshot:[43]

> After five months at the think tank I'd saved enough to buy some tools I needed, and quit. I was going to go into business fixing motorcycles ... the warehouse contained many decades' worth of abandoned detritus. You were forever discovering cool old stuff... This haphazard physical environment seemed better suited to inquiry than my sterile think tank office on K Street. The jumble of it supported a spirit of experimentation.

For Crawford the allure was machines, something that probably excites a good number of people, but I would suggest that this is a part of exploring nature in its widest sense: how things are, how they work, what is possible, and a key feature is "the *jumble* of it". In fact one of the beauties of the outdoors is that there are far fewer things to break or scratch or get upset about. Yes of course we can break and scratch and bruise bits of ourselves, but that happens anyway. For the Blackbird it is turning leaves, pulling up worms and exploring fallen logs; for us it is chopping logs, planting, harvesting, cooking, bottling, mending... It is time to accept that outsourcing such simple tasks has left us poorer people. Yes there are some things that professionals and businesses can do better, but we need to recover a sense that real work is good, not a chore. It keeps us alert and active and, surprisingly, our minds remain free to think. It is positive work, not just leisure that helps us find our wholeness, our vocation, our fulfilment. It is really no surprise that so many people want to work part-time, or that people work like stink when it comes to raising children or campaigning for positive change. We work at what we love. To do so is an act of worship, of loving God, who wants us to experience life in its fulness, not just with our minds and hearts but also with our strength.

# Chapter 14

# Roe Deer – integrating feminine and masculine

Roe Deer and Red Deer are the only species endemic to these islands. Fallow Deer were introduced by the Normans and the remaining species – Muntjac, Sika and Chinese Water Deer – were all introduced from East Asia in the past 100 years. Roe deer have been present from the end of the Palaeolithic period, nearly ten thousand years before Jesus taught in Galilee, and therefore before humans began farming.

Both of our native Deer species give us the benefit of two creatures in one, because they display such clear masculine and feminine aspects. In both the doe and stag we see grace and strength, agility and speed, gentleness and sensitivity, a sense of community and a sense of self. Yet they are very clearly doe and stag, each comfortable within their sex. Perhaps one of the lessons we can draw from the deer, then, is integration.

As individuals we can explore the two sides, masculine and feminine, which exist within each one of us, and discover how nebulous they can be. Within community we can also explore the roles of masculine and feminine, and perhaps there is room for exploratory play, especially as "gender" issues have become so politicized and, in a lot of situations, toxic.

It is too simple, I would even say misleading, to say feminine equals gentle, nurturing, cooperative whilst masculine equals tough, challenging, competitive. It is clear just by looking around that we are dealing with a subtle spectrum, a kaleidoscope even, and not clearly defined categories. Some women tend towards the masculine, some men towards the feminine, and they give rise to a multitude of different expressions. Most of us exist with a balance/tension, most often fairly clearly located within our own sex, but somehow there has grown an unhealthy sense of polarisation and opposition. Sexual preferences play into this too of course but let us not become distracted by that for now.

Both male and female Deer exhibit considerable poise, the kind of relaxed, self-contained alertness that is sought by dancers and those who practise martial arts. This ability to hold in tension the power to be still and to move swiftly without being tense is an aspect of integration. The Deer shares with the fox the ability to walk calmly through the forest seemingly without effort, despite the unevenness of ground thick with roots and undergrowth. They seem to be able to vanish, astonishing for such a large animal. Deer of both sexes are incredibly shy because, although their natural predators (Bear, Wolf, Lynx) have long gone, they retain the memory of them and the alertness and sensitivity of the hunted, no doubt assisted by the way humans continued where the others left off. So another thing they integrate into the present is a strong sense of the past, the story of their origins and many centuries of life. They remind us that our present time is in the context of a long and venerable history, and that we forget our story at our peril. Like the Fox they invite us to be sensitive to our environment, attuned to subtle signs that indicate what is healthy and what is to be avoided.

Roes do not live in herds, unlike Reds, but are either solitary or found in small family groups: a Doe and her offspring. They commonly give birth to twins or triplets in early summer (May and June). In medieval lore the Deer was a symbol of love, elusive and desirable, and poetry played on the concept of the hunt as a metaphor for eroticism and romance. This may be pure projection of course – nothing likes to be hunted, despite what some fools may claim – but we know that the musk of the stag is a powerfully arousing scent. So a creature who is at ease with her or his sexuality, sensitive, graceful and strong, able to hold himself or herself in perfect stillness and ready to move with incredible swiftness at a moment's notice. Spring is reasonably peaceful for the Roe, but things become more tense for the males towards the end of April when they begin to establish their territories and start to put on weight in the shoulders ready for rutting in early August.

A couple of simple actions will help these neighbours to thrive: driving more slowly and resisting the temptation to throw food out of the window. Even apple cores will make roadsides more attractive and therefore make collisions more likely. You can make yourself more "deer aware" by looking up the guidelines of the British Deer Society.[44] Roe Deer are not endangered but their preferred habitats (meadow and grasslands, field margins and woodlands) are all under threat. Wildlife-friendly farming is possible and we need to encourage the farming community to explore it further.

## From the Song of Solomon 1:2-4; 2:3, 6; 4:5-7, 11, 16; 5:4-5, 8 (NRSV)

*The lover: Let him kiss me with the kisses of his mouth! For your love is better than wine, your anointing oils are fragrant, your name is perfume poured out ... Draw me after you, let us make haste....*

*My beloved is to me a bag of myrrh that lies between my breasts.... With great delight I sat in his shadow, and his fruit was sweet to my taste.... O that his left hand were under my head, and that his right hand embraced me!...*

*The beloved: Your two breasts are like two fawns, twins of a gazelle, that feed among the lilies.... I will hasten to the mountain of myrrh and the hill of frankincense. You are altogether beautiful, my love; there is no flaw in you.... Your lips distil nectar, my bride; honey and milk are under your tongue...*

*The lover: Awake, O north wind, and come, O south wind! Blow*

*upon my garden that its fragrance may be wafted abroad. Let my*
*beloved come to his garden, and eat its choicest fruits.... My beloved*
*thrust his hand into the opening, and my inmost being yearned for*
*him. I arose to open to my beloved, and my hands dripped with*
*myrrh, my fingers with liquid myrrh, upon the handles of the bolt....*
*I am faint with love...*

## For reflection and prayer

In the film *The Name of the Rose*, a young novice monk has an
unexpected and powerful sexual encounter with a young woman.
The following verse is voiced over the scene as his older self looks
back:

*Who is this that looks forth like the dawn, fair as the moon, bright as*
*the sun, terrible as an army with banners?*
– Song of Solomon 6:10 (NRSV)

Christianity has not had an easy relationship with sex, but
perhaps that has been to do with the dominant culture rather
than just the teachings of churches. It is too easy to make the
latter the villain of the piece, when the reality is far more subtle
and complex. People have not properly understood Jesus'
celibacy, for example, or the part played by traditional values
which sought to protect young girls from unwanted pregnancy
and curb the natural lusts of young men. It must be remembered
that until quite recently pregnancy was a life-threatening
condition and therefore taken much more seriously than it is
today. Times have changed and it can seem that the Church has
not changed with them, that we are still "catching up". But one
thing remains that is of value: the love of God, and particularly
that aspect of it called compassion. Despite the fact that sex is
more obviously on show, we do not as a nation seem at ease with
it, able to integrate it into a healthy, balanced life. This may have
to do with other factors: the long hours we work; the compara-

tively sedentary, indoor life we live; the rapidity of new techno-logical advances; the decline of a common moral code and values. There has never been a more disorientating time to live in Britain. As well as the passionate verses quoted above, there is this:

> *This is my beloved and this is my friend.*
> – Song of Solomon 5:16 (NRSV)

We are called to *befriend* our desire, not to suppress it on the one hand or become controlled by it on the other. This is a long work, and requires patience, understanding and above all compassion. How can the Christian community create safe places within which this very vulnerable part of us can be properly explored? This has to be one of the messages that society is giving us: so many people want the Church to be a safe place, but they are shy, and quick to depart if they sense it is not.

# Chapter 15

# High Brown Fritillary – the slow work of God

The most endangered of Britain's fifty-nine native butterfly species, the High Brown Fritillary has seen massive population decline since the 1950s.[45] Once common, with populations throughout England and Wales, they occur naturally right across Europe, Asia and Japan, but in Britain are now found in only a handful of places. The largest population is in the north-west of England around Morecambe Bay, where at least three different charities are working together to preserve it. Large and powerful (her wingspan will be between 60 and 67mm), she begins to appear on the wing towards the end of June and into July, declining throughout August. Her larvae rely principally upon four species of violets for their food, but she feeds on a slightly wider range of other plants as well. These include thistles and knapweeds, Betony, Bramble, and Thyme. So she is found on grasslands, especially on south-facing slopes, at the edges of woodland, in coppices where these are not permitted to become overgrown (grazing animals in the wood being the traditional way of keeping vegetation down), limestone pavement and areas of mixed grass and bracken. Her roosting site therefore comes as a real surprise: right up in the tree canopy. Egg-laying females (there is only one generation born in each year) can be seen looking for violets in sunny, sheltered places, which are also ideal places for prayer. But she is very hard to spot and positively identify, so to see her is a true sign of grace.

The apparent flimsiness of butterflies makes us think again about appearances and where real resilience lies. The High Brown Fritillary has an individual range of about two kilometres. Proportionately that is similar to me flying from the

London Eye to Beaconsfield! So it is possible to live lightly *and* powerfully. More broadly this creature teaches us the important principle of "both/and" where we might otherwise be tempted to say "either/or".

Wouldn't it be great if we could allow more wild, unmanaged spaces (rewilding) and re-introduce traditional land management, especially coppicing woodlands? If this kind of large-scale thinking is beyond your means though, why not make room in your garden for butterfly-friendly, native plants such as wild primrose, violets, pansies and foxgloves (you can purchase seeds from some conservation charities) and cut out the use of pesticides? A lot of people immediately think "Buddleia" in relation to butterflies but in fact it is an exotic species from East Asia and invasive. Much better to let that clump of nettles remain (they are very easy to uproot if they start spreading too much – and they will). Bushy shrubs will also help by creating shelter from strong wind and Ivy (see separate chapter) provides roosts and places to lay eggs. Avoid peat composts, which come from fragile habitats where butterflies are endangered. Growing your own herbs will also attract butterflies as well as deepening your relationship with the living world: Parsley, Basil, Dill, Fennel and no doubt many others too. If you live near a concentration of High Brown Fritillaries then by all means do what you can to tempt them to you, but otherwise get a good field guide and enjoy the huge variety among these amazing creatures. And if you have the privilege of seeing a cocoon then simply watch and wait.

## From Ezekiel 37:1, 4-7 (NRSV)

*The hand of the Lord came upon me, and he brought me out by the spirit of the Lord and set me down in the middle of a valley; it was full of bones.... Then he said to me, "Prophesy to these bones, and say to them: O dry bones, hear the word of the Lord. Thus says the Lord*

*God to these bones: I will cause breath to enter you, and you shall*
*live. I will lay sinews on you, and will cause flesh to come upon you,*
*and cover you with skin, and put breath in you, and you shall live;*
*and you shall know that I am the Lord."*

*So I prophesied as I had been commanded...*

## For reflection and prayer

All butterflies are, of course, identified with personal transformation and a memorable, oft-quoted, story told by Nikos Kazantzakis reminds us that this has to be allowed to happen naturally.

"Above all, trust in the slow work of God...it is the law of all progress that it is made by passing through some stage of instability...accept the anxiety of feeling yourself in suspense and incomplete."
– Pierre Teilhard de Chardin.[46]

It takes a certain maturity to practise the call at the end of Psalm 27, to "Wait for the Lord", even if we are confident of seeing God's goodness. There are times in life when God seems to have departed, and our prayers can feel very sparse and empty. It can be tempting to give up and seek an easier way. Many people find at such times – which can be brought on by a difficult experience or some new experience or learning but also sometimes just happens – that their church actually seems to make matters more difficult. It can lead to a lot of questions and very few answers, and a sense that the answers given do not satisfy. All of this has to do with waiting on God, recognising that we need God to act, to take the initiative. This can also be true when we start something new believing God has called us. It is tempting to round up recruits and throw ourselves into publicity, but the problem with this is that it can leave little room for God to act, to call others naturally. A friend of mine is very rigorous about this, refusing to promote the idea he is exploring but rather waiting to be invited to present it. This includes waiting for people who have never heard of it to ask. Is this perverse? Perhaps, but if we believe in God then we have to trust that God will act. Otherwise the thing is just our own pet project, dry bones waiting for the breath of God to give them life. My spiritual director once told me "God wants to bring us to our wholeness by the shortest route possible", an encouragement to trust God's work not to try to accelerate it by our own, rather clumsy, means. Spending time outdoors, especially in pursuit of this creature, will teach you a deeper stillness. It does not come easily, so welcome it when it does come.

# Chapter 16

# Leopard Slug – an unlikely friend

On the morning I first wrote about Magpie I had just had a dream that featured slugs. In fact it was rather specific. I dreamt of a heap of slugs' eggs – something I've never seen to my knowledge – underneath an item of furniture I wanted to paint. This is not a book about dream interpretation, but if you want to offer one I'm all ears. I don't usually remember my dreams and was a bit put out that the first animal I dreamt about was slugs! So naturally I wrote about Magpie. In my defence I had thought about Magpie the day before, but enough excuses...

My own preferred term for Slugs is "night-crawlers", reflecting the fact that their main activity seems to be nocturnal, although they do not seem to have a clear diurnal pattern and this in itself suggests that they may represent the occupation of more than one world. In the same way the teacher Jesus spoke about "the Kingdom of God", which exists beside, within and beyond the world we know. Being hermaphrodite, it isn't really appropriate to use the terms "he" and "she" for Slug, another way in which different worlds are brought together in this extra-ordinary creature.

There are many slugs that are native to the UK, and several invasive species too. This one – the Leopard Slug, is more benign than most. He has to do with decay and being large, slimy and unattractive he is not greatly loved; regardless of this he ploughs relentlessly onward, following paths that make little sense to us. His home is the compost heap, the leaf litter, wherever there is damp and comparative warmth (he becomes active whenever the temperature rises above 5°C). Like Whales he has some kind of inner method of navigation which remains mysterious to us. Sometimes, when many are seen together, a pattern may be discerned, but even when he is not visible the silvery trail he leaves is evidence of his passing.

I will confess I was reluctant to write about Slugs. I actually feared what they might have to tell me. But it was this fear that told me to push ahead. Fear is not to be trusted. The opposite of faith, it causes our spiritual awareness to contract and is all too often self-fulfilling. Evidence from recent archaeology on the islands of Orkney shows that Neolithic peoples included a huge midden near their main place of worship.[47] Analysis suggests that this was more than mere laziness; that decay was important to them and even honoured as essential to new life. Today we have created a life that removes us from decay and treats it as something disgusting and unhygienic. And yet a properly-managed compost heap does not smell and produces a rich, healthy fertility that is a benefit to any garden. You can literally grow your dinner in it! And Leopard Slug, who does not attack living plants, will leave it all for you. His diet is dead, rotting vegetation and other slugs, including those that would help themselves to your salad. He may not look attractive but he is invaluable in the process of cycling nutrients, a benefit to your garden rather than a pest. Any life lived in harmony with the environment will have an honoured place for decomposition and perhaps this is one of the many gifts that Leopard Slug can give to us, if we will allow.

So what should we do for him? Probably nothing much. They exist in far greater numbers than most of us would care to know about. However, our use of poisons to neutralize them probably leads to all kinds of collateral damage (birds eating slug pellets being the most obvious) and if their large numbers do suggest something is out of balance, how far do we really have to look for the reason? If, like me, you have been surprised to discover that there is a slug that will actually protect your raised bed or field crop from predators, then it is clear there is a considerable work of education to be done. There aren't many slug champions in the world, so how about it?

## From Jonah 1:1-4, 10-12 (NRSV)

*Now the word of the Lord came to Jonah son of Amittai, saying, "Go at once to Nineveh, that great city, and cry out against it; for their wickedness has come up before me." But Jonah set out to flee to Tarshish from the presence of the Lord. He went down to Joppa and found a ship going to Tarshish; so he paid his fare and went on board, to go with them to Tarshish, away from the presence of the Lord.*

*But the Lord hurled a great wind upon the sea, and such a mighty storm came upon the sea that the ship threatened to break up....*

*The men knew that [Jonah] was fleeing from the presence of the Lord, because he had told them so. Then they said to him, "What shall we do to you, that the sea may quiet down for us?" He said to them, "Pick me up and throw me into the sea; then the sea will quiet down for you; for I know it is because of me that this great storm has come upon you."*

## For reflection and prayer

The trail Slug leaves behind serves a number of purposes. It is a form of excretion, enabling him to shed toxins and particles that would otherwise block his internal organs. It enables free movement across rough surfaces. It acts like Theseus' ball of wool, helping him to retrace his "steps" (really one elongated step, since the whole animal is basically a muscular foot). It absorbs water which aids his sense of smell and has a fibrous quality that enables vertical climbing. And to our eyes its silvery reflectivity lends a sense of magic and mystery to this creature of many worlds.

We too can find that the very thing that assists us can leave a trail that marks and affects others. Jonah is a prime example of this. His avoidance of the powerful forces in his own life led to chaos for everyone else.[48] It is only when he took responsibility that peace returned and the result (if you read on) is that others were converted, not by being "evangelised" but because of their own openness and the experience they had of God.

Are we aware of the things we excrete into the world, the way we mark our passing? Sometimes there are habits that are helpful to us but which are not necessarily pleasing to others. I am not suggesting we have to set about "fixing" this, but simply asking for the grace of awareness. *We are also that which we fear ourselves to be*, even though that is not the whole story.

Get hold of some compost (please avoid peat-based ones though, which come from fragile ecosystems) and work it through your fingers. It contains nutrients that have been made available for you by others, nutrients that you cannot access without the help of yet more others. Take time to let this physical contact affect you, and observe how you respond to it.

# Chapter 17

# Rosebay Willowherb – life on the margins

What an eye-opener researching this book has been! I found the following on a website that shall remain nameless, entitled "Creating a Wild Flower Meadow":

> *Traditionally, wild flower meadows were hay meadows which were cut during the summer for hay and used for grazing over the winter. They consisted of wild rather than cultivated grasses with a large variety of other native flowering plants. Their value lay in the diversity of their plant life which provided food and shelter for many different invertebrate species which in turn meant that there was an abundance of food for birds and mammals. The plant species composition varied from area to area depending on geological, soil and climatic conditions....*
>
> *Wild flowers will not be able to compete well in areas of lush weed growth, so it is important to start out with a completely weed-free site. This can be achieved by either digging out any existing plants or using a weedkiller such as glyphosate. It may be necessary to repeat these activities over a period to ensure the area is clear.*

Yes, folks, to create a *wild* meadow it is deemed necessary to blitz the land with poison several times to remove all the "weeds"! Fortunately not everyone who wants to see wild flowers make a comeback takes this anthropocentric view. In fact a huge number of wild flowering plants native to the UK are what might be called "weeds", the definition of which is anything that grows where a human being does not want it. Surely it is not for us to "create" wild places. In fact despite all our knowledge we still seem unable to grasp this simple point: nature does not need us to control and manage her. Keith Skene made this point brilliantly in a talk[49] delivered at the Greenbelt Festival in 2012: "If you plant trees in a field you don't get a forest. What you get is a field of trees". We have an example of just such a field within 20 minutes of where I live. It is a very strange and not altogether healthy place.

Rosebay Willowherb, by way of contrast, is a fine example of what nature can do if left to her own devices. Known in other parts of the world as "Fireweed" (there's that weed thing again) because she quickly colonises land after a fire, she is tall and striking, with delicate pink flowers that belie her hardiness. These appear from June to September in a spiked crown supported by a strong central stem from which thin, blade-like leaves spiral upwards. Her name derives from the shape of these leaves, which are very like those of Willow trees. She will be around one metre and a half in height. Originally a pioneer of woodland clearings, this creature has profited from human activity and can be seen in all kinds of places, especially where scarcity of water prohibits other plants from gaining so rapid a foothold. Road and railway verges are favourites as well as woodland rides and footpaths. After a storm she springs up among the fallen giants and quickly gives the impression that she is taking over. But this is not the case. Despite being perennial,[50] she does give way to other species and, left alone, the land slowly reverts to forest again. She cannot survive in the shade but, through her pollen and her seed, she lives and moves on. The seeds are not unlike those of Thistles, tiny dots sporting a mass of light, feathery down, ideally suited to drift on the vagrant breezes of the British countryside. Each individual can release up to eighty thousand such seeds in a single season.

So what can we do for Rosebay Willowherb? Make tea from the leaves and/or flowers, scoop the pith from the stem to add to soups, use the downy seeds to get your wood fire started. This is not the kind of advice I am giving for all wild creatures, but this one is nowhere near endangered and is one of the gifts of nature to her children. This kind of use draws us nearer to the environment of which we are a part. It helps reduce our dependence upon beverages imported from distant lands and paraffin-based firelighters, both of which greatly increase our Carbon footprint. Delight in the ethereal beauty of the drifting seeds which speak to us of our own temporariness and pilgrimage (Hildegard of Bingen once described herself as "a feather on the breath of God"), allow her to coax you away from the road to the verge and beyond, and let her grow where she grows. She does no harm.

## From Mark 2:13-17 (NRSV)

*Jesus went out again beside the sea; the whole crowd gathered around him, and he taught them. As he was walking along, he saw Levi son of Alphaeus sitting at the tax booth, and he said to him, "Follow me." And he got up and followed him. And as he sat at dinner in Levi's house, many tax collectors and sinners were also sitting with Jesus and his disciples—for there were many who followed him. When the scribes of the Pharisees saw that he was eating with sinners and tax collectors, they said to his disciples, "Why does he eat with tax collectors and sinners?" When Jesus heard this, he said to them, "Those who are well have no need of a physician, but those who are sick; I have come to call not the righteous but sinners."*

## For reflection and prayer

Describing something as "weedy" usually indicates a kind of flimsy weakness combined with a straggly ugliness. I have yet to hear this term used as a compliment. In fact almost the exact opposite is true: most "weeds" are as tough as nails, able to survive in nutrient-poor environments, often with little rainfall or drainage that is so free it amounts to the same thing. They hold together soils that would otherwise be washed away (especially if the glyphosphate gang are given their head) and provide food and shelter to myriads of tiny creatures who in turn support larger ones. And, as our friend the Rosebay Willowherb so ably demonstrates, there is great beauty in wildness. But then human beings seem to be very intolerant when it comes to aesthetics, generally regarding a tiny minority of their own kind as beautiful and persecuting those whose natural shape is outside a fairly narrow set of parameters.

Mark's Gospel shows Jesus, at the very start of his ministry, reclining[51] amongst the weeds, at home with those who were on the fringes of society. In Britain we have done our level best to squeeze nature out, despite the fact that our own existence depends entirely upon nature. Indeed it makes better sense to say that we exist *within* nature. There is no existence outside of it. So what exactly are we communicating about our self-understanding when we describe a particular – usually very small – area as a "nature reserve"? It makes me think of those Native Americans who were herded onto reservations, kept on the margins by a people who never bothered to really understand them, much less adopt their millennia-old relationship with the land. Rosebay Willowherb seems to me to be what we could call a "spiritual indicator" species. Cropping up in the interstices created by an overdeveloped society, quietly but persistently standing as a witness that life will not be contained or controlled. See the light filtering through the leaves and petals in the early morning, swaying gently as cars rush by, their oblivious occupants tuned into human affairs and entertainments. Sense the gentle invitation and welcome characteristic of Christ, his habit of avoiding the wealthy, the powerful and the popular. Even (especially?) dying on the cross, there were many who would have simply passed him by, not even looking, on their way into and out of the busy city. We like to believe that he was always central, but the Gospels do not tell it like that. The "centre" (Rome) was over two thousand kilometres (more than fourteen hundred miles) away. Jesus did not go there. He did not even die in the centre of Jerusalem, and when he was in the corridors of power he observed a resolute, though not absolute, silence. If we are to find life we need to be where Christ is, at the margins, among the unexpected. In Britain today there are many who are spiritually alive, and lively, but they will not thrive in the shade cast by the Church.

## Chapter 18

# White-berried Mistletoe – truth hidden in plain sight

Native to Northern Europe but also occurring naturally in parts of Asia, he is instantly recognisable by his olive green leaves and network of branches. What we call Mistletoe is in fact one of a family of mistletoes that comprises around fifteen hundred different species, mostly within the subtropical and tropical belts. He is described by the Woodland Trust[52] as "semi-parasitic" because as well as creating sugars from sunlight like all green plants he also extracts certain nutrients from his host tree. This is most commonly cultivated Apple varieties, Oak and Hawthorn but he can also be seen on Limes, Poplars, Maple, Willow, Crab Apple.... in fact he has the widest range of host species of any of the world's Mistletoes. We seem to have a huge population in Cheltenham, very much in evidence during the winter months, and I only found out through researching this book that the Cotswolds stand at the eastern edge of Mistletoe's main concentration in the UK, centred around South East Wales as far north as the Clee Hills and with an outpost in North Somerset.[53]

Once thought of as something of a pest, it is only in recent years that his value to all manner of wildlife has been recognised. He is now regarded as vital to a wide variety of creatures and may, for that reason, be helpful in regenerating woodlands that have become denuded through overcropping or disease.[54] Having said that he generally prefers isolated trees rather than woods. It may even be that humans' habit of creating clearings and then extending these so that now we have only a tiny proportion left of the great forests that once dominated the landscape has actually led to a far greater abundance than would have occurred naturally.

His berries, though poisonous to some animals, are food for the Blackcap, and she assists his propagation by her habit of cleaning her beak on the barks of trees, depositing the seeds in the process and so assisting in distribution. The rather more obviously-named Mistle Thrush is actually less effective at spreading the seeds because she swallows the whole berry, seeds and all, and fewer of these find their way onto tree bark as a result. But because he makes such use of birds, including Redwings, Waxwings and Fieldfares, Mistletoe does not bother giving off a scent, unlike other flowering plants. He is also significant for a small number of insects. Of these perhaps the most obvious is the Mistletoe Marble Moth, who lays her eggs on him in July and August.[55] The larvae tunnel into the stems and then await the following spring when they extend their tunnels and eventually emerge and pupate in June. Even the deciduous leaves play a part, making an important addition to the leaf-litter on the forest floor.[56] Research in Australia has shown that removing Mistletoe from an ecosystem can dramatically reduce biodiversity.[57] But since this concerned a different species from our native variety, there is scope for a similar research project to be carried out in the UK. Any takers?

If you can see flowers then he is at least five years old. It probably took most of his first year of life to penetrate the host tree and develop the structure through which he extracts her nutrients. His action will weaken her but not kill, and when she dies he will too. Being evergreen he is brought into the house with holly and ivy around Christmastime. His berries, rich with sticky white syrup, have long been associated with sex and fertility. So he was worn by young women to attract a husband (the tradition of kissing under Mistletoe probably stems from this) and was even used in medicines intended to overcome impotence. One of his alternative names is "All-heal" (something he, somewhat confusingly, shares with several other plants) because he has been used to treat a wide variety of complaints and there is some evidence to suggest that he can assist the body's natural attempts to fight cancer. In any event he has been very important to Druidic practice and plays a significant role in folklore generally.

The national picture for this species is very patchy. Rare in some places and possibly too abundant in others, simply placing Mistletoe seeds on an apple tree in your garden is probably enough to ensure one establishes there (you do not need to injure the tree) but it may not be sufficient to help conserve the species. If you are buying Mistletoe, make sure it is from a sustainable source, such as the "Mistletoe Campaign" being run by the National Trust.[58] Ask your local supplier where their Mistletoe comes from. If it is imported encourage them to source it more locally. Support small apple, juice and cider producers (which is a good thing to do anyway) and think about going to the great Mistletoe Festival in Tenbury Wells[59] which is always at the beginning of December, a great way to begin the countdown to Christmas.

## From Mark 4:2-3, 21, 26, 31, 34 (NRSV)

*He began to teach them many things in parables, and in his teaching he said to them:*

*"Listen! A sower went out to sow...."*
*"Is a lamp brought in to be put ... under the bed?*
*"The kingdom of God is as if someone would scatter seed on the ground...*
*"It is like a mustard seed...*

*...he did not speak to them except in parables, but he explained everything in private to his disciples.*

## For reflection and prayer

The fourth chapter of Mark's Gospel has been significant to me for a number of years now. It contains a profound paradox. On the one hand Jesus seems to saying that God's Kingdom will spread throughout the earth: in the story of the sower (verses 1 to 9) the "seed" (the message) of the Kingdom lands in all kinds of different places; in the story of the lamp (verses 21 to 23) the light fills the whole house; in the stories of the wheat and the mustard seed (verses 26 to 32) it grows to fulness. But at the same time he also tells us that it is hidden: not everyone will respond, perhaps even the majority will either lose hold of it or never receive it in the first place. He does not seem to think this is a bad thing, speaking to the crowd yet separated from them, never quite in the same place as those he calls.

How does this compare with churches that describe themselves as "a visible presence in the community", or clergy who hold "significant" roles in secular organisations? What Jesus describes seems to be much more like the Mistletoe – organic, spreading, generous, connected, providing, supporting, misunderstood, uninvited, unexpected – than the large, visible organisations and structures that claim to represent him. We are living in a period when it is increasingly clear that there are really two churches: one an unpredictable, organic movement that spans the globe and history; the other a set of institutions with rules and hierarchies that are struggling to adapt to the times. Of course the hope is that there will be considerable overlap between the two, and some no doubt struggle to see beyond the confines of their local expression of this thing called "church" (a word which, incidentally, Jesus hardly used at all), but there is also considerable tension. The Mistletoe embodies the paradox of the Kingdom: without him life becomes impoverished, unsustainable, meaningless, and yet he is unassuming and depends upon those in whom he can take root.

## Chapter 19

# Honey Bee – complexity, cooperation, communication and congruence

Her ancestry dates back millions of years and yet her lifespan is only about six weeks. This starts when the Queen lays an egg in one of the cells of the honeycomb. She hatches out as a larva (looking like a tiny maggot) three days later and continues to grow, shedding her skin five times. She then pupates and in nine days emerges as an adult "worker", making her first excursion around three weeks later. She will never sleep, but will conserve energy by remaining motionless overnight. Her first flight will usually be in the company of hundreds of others who have hatched at the same time. They will spend some time outside, facing the nest, while they orientate themselves. They also use this opportunity to void their faeces (resulting in little orange spots all over the clothes of anyone who is enjoying the spectacle). Her wings work at an incredible speed, around two hundred beats per second, generating the distinctive buzzing we associate with this creature, and carrying her up to ten kilometres if needed. That is unusual though: she generally remains within a couple of kilometres of home. She can reach speeds of nearly 30 Km/h (this speed is roughly halved when she is returning carrying her burden of nectar, water or pollen). She has five eyes, which give her a highly developed visual awareness, and she sees mostly at the blue end of the spectrum, including ultraviolet, well beyond our visual range. She can even see the Sun on a cloudy or foggy day because she is sensitive to polarized light. It would appear that she navigates using four criteria: smell, visual clues (landmarks and the position of the sun), an awareness of time, and a sense of the earth's magnetic field. In addition she clearly has a capacity for memory, calculation and communication (see below). So perhaps the first thing she reminds us of is complexity: simple answers may be attractive, but they can be misleading. Life is often more complex than it may appear, and there is always more to learn.

Invaluable as a pollinator (it is reckoned that about a third of what we eat relies upon her) her kind have long served human purposes, and yet despite this she remains essentially a wild animal. Although it is likely that the majority of colonies are being housed by beekeepers in the UK, I have seen wild colonies in Warwickshire and South Wales, and I am confident they exist elsewhere too. Her honey is a real "super-food", containing a range of essential minerals, vitamins and enzymes, and of course energy in the form of natural sugars. It is easy for us to forget that it is not made for our consumption, but is a vital food supply to keep the colony throughout the winter. During the dark months there is almost no external food available and the low temperatures prevent outdoor activity. Yet the colony does not hibernate, remaining active all year round.

As impressive as all the above statistics are (and it has been quite a discipline not to ramble on for pages and pages), the lesson I want to draw from the honey bee is something I am going to call "embodied communication". For centuries we have known about the mysterious "waggle dance", but it was only in 1973 that Karl Ritter von Frisch finally managed to decode some of what it signifies. It would appear that the dance communicates the location of a food source in terms of direction and the time it takes to fly there (the dancer takes into account the position of the Sun and the wind speed and direction, allowing for the relative movement of the Sun in the time it takes to return to the hive with the news). So we see here a tiny creature who embodies an amazing array of skills, one who is very aware of where she is and where she is going, who shares this knowledge with her colony through her life and movement, and who gives life not only to them but to many other creatures as well, including us.

## From Matthew 7:15, 19-20, 21 (NRSV)

*Beware of false prophets, who come to you in sheep's clothing but inwardly are ravenous wolves.... Every tree that does not bear good fruit is cut down and thrown into the fire. Thus you will know them by their fruits.*

*Not everyone who says to me, 'Lord, Lord,' will enter the kingdom of heaven, but only the one who does the will of my Father in heaven.*

## For reflection and prayer

The dance of the honey bee reminds us that we are called to be aware of what we embody. Whatever we claim to believe, the way we live and behave will communicate far more effectively than our words. In a few chapters' time we will be considering the value of reticence and this applies not only to what we take in but also what we give out. I well remember attending a particular annual Christian conference several years ago. The words were all about the grace of God, the love of God and the desire of God to rescue us. But what came across most forcefully was a kind of indignant anger, a harshness that jarred almost tangibly. In counselling this is called "incongruence", when the words do not match the "harmony". Those who have studied such things tell us that an awful lot of human communication is non-verbal: body-language, attitude, eye contact, the genuineness of facial expressions, proximity – all these "speak" and they can give away very clearly whether we really mean what we say. Could it be that we (Christians) have been too vocal about such things as love, joy, peace, patience, kindness, generosity, faithfulness, gentleness, and self-control (Galatians 5:22-23)? Perhaps it is time to recognise – and be more honest about – the fact that Jesus' "Church" is something we are *becoming* as much as what we already are. And so it may be that, like the honey bee, before we are able to effectively speak we must first learn to dance.[60]

## Chapter 20

# Pipistrelle – embracing our shadow

There are eighteen native species of bat in Britain, of which the most common – and also the smallest – is the Pipistrelle. In fact he is now called the Common Pipistrelle since it was discovered in the 1990s that what we thought was one species is in fact two: the Common and the Soprano. Their calls – at 45 kHz and 55 kHz respectively – are what gave the game away, and those who have been inducted into the strange world of bat detecting will know all about that. If you have not been yet, find out where your nearest bat group is and go. Bats represent between one quarter and one third of all mammal species in Britain and in 2008 six species were chosen to be indicators of biodiversity in the UK.[61] They are the only mammals that are capable of flight, which uses a lot of energy. As a result a single bat can eat up to three thousand insects in a single hunt.

The value of bat droppings is so great that, in 1890, the King of Siam had his personal seal placed at the entrance of around twenty caves in recognition.[62] In other countries bats are the only pollinators of certain plants important to humans.[63] They are extremely adaptable. The Greater Horseshoe, for example, is a natural cave-dweller who found a new home in the roofs of old houses. At one time there may have been as many as fifteen thousand at a single site, but their populations declined rapidly in the twentieth century and their range is a shadow of what it once was.

Traditionally people have feared bats and so they can represent the things we want to hide away from, especially the violence in ourselves. Able to find their way flawlessly in the dark, and to locate small, fast-moving prey, the Bat stands for sensitivity and awareness, sociability, family and the importance of physical touch to communicate love. The cave-dwelling species in particular remind us of rebirth, entering the earth, like Christ himself, to re-emerge again. They hibernate throughout the winter months and will only begin to emerge in March when temperatures begin to rise and insects start to appear. Therefore their appearance in any numbers most years coincides with the celebration of Easter.

Pipistrelle reminds us of community because of the way they roost together, and of family, which always exists within the wider group. Because he emerges at around sunset he stands for the in-between times in life, when we see less clearly and need to develop other senses than those we have relied upon in the past. And of course, like many native British animals, he teaches us that darkness is to be accepted and embraced so that we can move more freely, accepting that we are a mixture of light and shade but fully loved by God.

What can we do for them? Restore their habitat, especially roosting sites, by allowing trees to mature, preserving mature trees and installing bat boxes (see below) in woodland. Reduce the use of pesticides and generally encourage insects in gardens and other areas, and encourage those we know to hold a positive image of them.

Although in general I prefer natural to artificial interventions, I see bat boxes as a step in the right direction. It seems unlikely that we will allow our woods to restore themselves as extensively as we need for health, and so bat boxes are a short-term, limited way of restoring the balance. They also enable us to study and therefore better understand these much maligned neighbours.

## Matthew 9:9-13 (NRSV)

*As Jesus was walking along, he saw a man called Matthew sitting at the tax booth; and he said to him, "Follow me." And he got up and followed him. And as he sat at dinner in the house, many tax collectors and sinners came and were sitting with him and his disciples. When the Pharisees saw this, they said to his disciples, "Why does your teacher eat with tax collectors and sinners?" But when he heard this, he said, "Those who are well have no need of a physician, but those who are sick. Go and learn what this means, 'I desire mercy, not sacrifice.' For I have come to call not the righteous but sinners."*

## For reflection and prayer

The Pharisees – and probably some of the disciples too – had good reason to question Jesus' choice in calling Matthew. And yet Jesus chooses to embrace those who are unacceptable in his society. Perhaps you can think of other times when he does this. But how do I respond to those who are hard to accept? Can I name them before God and pray for them? What about the parts of me that I turn away from? Is it possible that these too have a value of which I am presently unaware?

How about your own night vigil? Find a place where there are likely to be bats (anywhere with a good number of trees and a body of water) about fifteen to twenty minutes after sunset and wait. Ask for the grace of awareness. Be vigilant, watching their flight until the darkness makes further watching impossible or they seem to have gone. Write down your thoughts in your journal, but don't force anything if nothing comes. Repeat as you sense the need!

# Chapter 21

# Ivy – joyfulness in creation

Ever since moving to my present home I have been confronted with the Green Man. He stares enigmatically at me across the road, with an unreadable expression. Many would say that this is a normal property of Ivy, whose tendency to create a curtain of leaves means that all sorts of shapes and patterns can be discerned, just as we can do when staring at the clouds. But how often do you take time to do this? It is good for the brain to drift sometimes, to let connections happen spontaneously. Apart from anything else, we are clearly not meant to be productive all the time. I am well aware that the "face" I see is partly of my own making. If I look along the hedge I can see all sorts of faces, some menacing, some comical. But there is a reason – perhaps more than one – that this face draws me again and again.

The hedge I am looking at, at the time of writing, may be doomed. There are plans to create a bus lane which will widen the road on the other side of it, and that may mean a significant reduction in what one of the proposal documents dismissively refers to as "foliage". As you can tell, I am opposed to the scheme, but that is not my point here. It is the way nature is looking back at me, a member of a species that has become very skilled at living out of balance, out of harmony, with our environment. The expression on this "face", as I have said, is inscrutable. I sense a seriousness and a strength, an awareness coupled with a total lack of fear. Nature is not threatened by our activity, but what we do may have consequences in nature that turn to bite us. We harm ourselves if we fail to see this.

Ivy – "Ifig" in Old English – is a slow-growing climber that occurs all over Europe, from Ukraine to Ireland, from Sweden to Cyprus. She has also been unhelpfully introduced to the USA and New Zealand. When not wrapping herself around trees, walls and anything else that gets in the way, she spreads along at ground level, shading out grasses and other ground-layer plants. As she matures she forms tough, yet flexible, woody stems with countless root-like "holdfasts" that anchor her to the climbing surface, but she is epiphytic rather than parasitic (in other words she grows on other things but takes no sustenance from them). Native to Britain, she is clearly a creature of the extensive woodland that used to exist unbroken from east to west and into which humans came to create first clearings, then fields and finally what some have recently described as a kind of rural desert landscape. Ivy has taken these changes in her stride, and is far from the only species to do so. Incredibly tough and adaptable, she can cope with most types of soil, light and shade, heat and cold. She features in Christmas Carols and winter folklore because she is one of the few green things in the frosted landscape at that time of year, although the darkness of her leaves strikes a more sombre note than the bright greens of spring.

Very late in the year the Ivy comes into flower and it is then that she exhibits, for those who are alert, her extraordinary power. A more understated flower is hard to find. Light green, like a cluster of little green balls on the ends of stubby stems, you can easily miss it, although you will be aware of a thick, heady, honey-like scent that is at once entrancing and yet not altogether pleasant. Some people find this smell deeply arousing, though not all, but its effect on other creatures is palpable. When these flowers appear it is as if every kind of insect has decided, for a day or two, to have a "bee day", collecting the nectar with greedy gusto, and indeed honey bees often use it as a vital late-season supplement.[64] The feasting goes on into the night as moths also get in on the action. The knock-on effect is that bats have a feast of their own, of course, so it is as if Ivy has thrown a huge party just before the onset of winter, something humans have traditionally done as well. The benefit to the plant is pollination, and over the cold period the flowers give way to the blackening fruit, which is itself a vital food source for Thrush, Pigeon, Blackbird and no doubt many others, and these in turn spread the seeds which pass through their digestive tracts unharmed. Many birds nest in her as well, and some rely upon the insect life she supports, so as unassuming as she may seem, Ivy is a vital part of the British wildscape.

Take the prunings to decorate your house for Christmas. It does the plant no real harm (her roots are deep and almost impossible to extract, especially if she has dug into the base of a stone wall or the root system of a tree – she will be back!) and it means you are not joining in the mass destruction caused by the production of vast quantities of plastic tat. Ivy is not even slightly endangered, so perhaps there is nothing much we need to do for her really, but like all things she has her place. She was here before we were so let us consider, before we root her out, what else is being discarded when we do so. It is not a plant you are looking at: she is a whole garden in herself.

## From Matthew 11:2-5, 7, 18-19 (NRSV)

*When John heard in prison what the Messiah was doing, he sent word by his disciples and said to him, "Are you the one who is to come, or are we to wait for another?" Jesus answered them, "Go and tell John what you hear and see: the blind receive their sight, the lame walk, the lepers are cleansed, the deaf hear, the dead are raised, and the poor have good news brought to them."*

*As they went away, Jesus began to speak to the crowds about John: "...John came neither eating nor drinking, and they say, 'He has a demon'; the Son of Man came eating and drinking, and they say, 'Look, a glutton and a drunkard, a friend of tax collectors and sinners!'..."*

## For reflection and prayer

If you saw ivy draped over a branch outside a house in ancient Rome it meant that alcohol was being sold there. This tradition carried on into Medieval Europe, including Britain, where it was referred to as an "alestake". So Ivy is the great party host and is rightly associated with festivity. In our own time Christians are keen to recover a joyfulness that centuries of more austere spiritualities appear to lack. In fact the answer is not to do away with fasting and seriousness, as true spirituality is not trivial but has to do with a complete understanding of well-being. This must surely include the ability to laugh and love and let go of our cares. After all, the invitation is to an eternal party! One of the ways our lives have got out of balance is that our parties can be terribly destructive, but the answer is not to abolish parties. Rather it is to rediscover a joyfulness in creation and the many ways in which we can dance in time and in tune with the world around us. And if sometimes the dancing gets a bit wild and out of hand, why worry? What happens in a single evening does not have to set the scene for the whole of life. So even when you are fasting, don't forget to start planning the party: the bridegroom is coming!

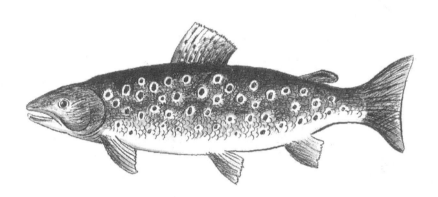

## Chapter 22

# Grey Seal – listening to the heart

Like us, he can move between worlds – the land and the water – and also like us he naturally favours one over the other. So we could regard him as a kind of mirror-image of ourselves. He stares back at us with contemplative curiosity, a peaceful and social creature who moves clumsily enough on dry ground but in the ocean acquires the elegance and power of the most accomplished dancer.

He has long been a creature of myth: in the Scottish islands appearing as the seductive Selkie, who casts off his magical outer skin (which gives to its wearer the power to inhabit the neritic realm) to reveal his human shape and dance on the moonlit sand or stretch out on warm rocks to soak up the sun's rays. Beautiful to behold and sensuous lovers, they could be captured, trapped in human form, by any who could seize and hide these skins. And so it was that many local stories were woven around island hearths in deep winter, and no doubt many an eye stared lost in thought in the firelight in a reverie of desire. For the Selkies were male and female, and had no understanding of their allure to human souls.

Are the Selkies merely the projections of small, isolated communities where opportunities for love were rare; where virgins and marriages were vigorously protected; where labour was hard and life was short? Or do they point to another way to look upon these nearby strangers, who seem to share an understanding with us across the rippling waves and limpet-encrusted rocks? These are themes explored by others better versed in sea lore than I, but if you want to explore them further why not get in touch?

Of the thirty-three species of Seal that exist worldwide, only two are native to Britain: the Common and the Grey. We are privileged to play host to around forty per cent of the global population. There are three main concentrations: the Eastern Atlantic (95 per cent of this population are found around our coasts), the Baltic and on the Northern coastline of North America. To give you an idea of numbers, at the start of the breeding season in 2000 the global population was around 310,000 individuals, so it's no exaggeration to say they are one of the world's rarest Seals.

Our friend is a mature male, at least three years old, and is noticeably bigger and darker than his female contemporaries. Around 2.6 m (8'6"), he weighs about 350 Kg (just over 55 stone). If he manages to avoid death by predation, illness or accident (getting entangled in fishing nets or what one website euphemistically calls "marine debris") he may live to be around 40 years old. In all this time he will remain within 80Km (50 miles) of home. So, like others in these meditations, he embodies a paradox: living at sea, which for us immediately suggests freedom and distance; he seems to be intensely rooted.

He spends two thirds of his year in the water, staying out for up to three weeks at a time, feeding mainly on fish of many different species, although he seems to prefer those that live near the sea floor such as Sandeels, Pollock and Mackerel. He is capable of diving to between 30m and 70m and can hold his breath for an impressive nine minutes; although most dives are about three minutes long (his nostrils actually relax shut). Despite the absence of external ears he has excellent hearing (females and their pups recognise each other's voices, which make the breeding colony a very noisy experience) and very sensitive whiskers. As a pup weighing only 14 Kg (31 lbs), he had about a fifty per cent chance of survival, and was utterly dependent upon his mother's milk for his first four weeks. That milk was a rich mix though: 60 per cent fat, so he packed on the pounds quickly enough. After a month he began to wean and quickly lost his furry "lanugo". This coincided with the following mating season, so one of his earliest experiences would have been avoiding getting crushed by fighting males!

October is when mating begins, when he and his fellows will come ashore in vast numbers to form "rookeries" (unlike the much smaller Common, or Harbour, Seals who mate offshore). Ironically this makes him the largest mammal to mate on land in the UK. The largest rookeries occur in the Hebrides, Orkney, the Isle of May (which lies 8 Km off the coast of Fife), the Farne Islands (off the coast of Northumberland – the tide decides how many of these there are at any given time) and Donna Nook Nature reserve in Lincolnshire. Of these sites the single most important is in the Outer Hebrides, a group of islands called Heisker, off the west coast of North Uist, where about 20 per cent of the total population of pups are born each year. The last humans left Heisker in the 1940s and in 1966 it was designated a National Nature Reserve. There is no ban on hunting these creatures but it is illegal to do so without a licence and the UK government policy since the late 1970s has been not to issue any. Despite this he consistently chooses to avoid human settlements. Could this be because of a long folk memory of bloodier times?

## From Matthew 16:24-28 (NRSV)

*Then Jesus told his disciples, "If any want to become my followers, let them deny themselves and take up their cross and follow me. For those who want to save their life will lose it, and those who lose their life for my sake will find it. For what will it profit them if they gain the whole world but forfeit their life? Or what will they give in return for their life?*

*"For the Son of Man is to come with his angels in the glory of his Father, and then he will repay everyone for what has been done. Truly I tell you, there are some standing here who will not taste*

*death before they see the Son of Man coming in his kingdom."*

## For reflection and prayer

"God commanded us to love our neighbours and our enemies," wrote G.K. Chesterton, "because all too often they are the same people". We see this time and again in human societies, but what a tragedy that we have become an enemy to so many of our neighbours, who have no enmity towards us. Most of us love Seals at first sight, floating upright in the water with dark eyes trained upon us, seeming to invite us to join them. Historically we have treated them appallingly, regarding them – as we do with so many creatures – purely in terms of monetary value whilst congratulating ourselves on being the only creature with a soul and a sense of civilisation.

If this seems hopelessly sentimental, perhaps it is worth considering a different challenge to our economic sensibilities. It is now clear that huge reserves of oil, gas and coal exist that we must leave alone if we are to avoid catastrophic climate change. These reserves could provide jobs and income and energy to power all kinds of "progress" and "development". They are a resource that would benefit us hugely – so we are told by the people who are waiting, poised with extraction technology and dollar signs in their eyes. And the challenge is to leave it in the ground.

Does this sound strange, unrealistic, hopelessly naive? If it does then I would suggest that we need to take a look at our culture. "Culture", as Bishop Graham Cray has said, "is what we think is obvious. It is the stuff that we know without having to think about it". The difficulty facing us, then, and not for the first time, is not the facts but our habits. And perhaps the worst of these is that we tend to work out *how* to do things with barely a pause to consider whether we *should*. The world as we know it is utterly riddled with a capitalist ideal. Try being the person who says "Haven't we got enough?" at any political gathering and you will quickly see what I mean. But at some point we have to realise that relentless, eternal economic growth is simply unsustainable. At some point we have to start identifying what is "enough", and we have to allow room so that others have enough too.

But there is a danger here. It would be all too easy to suggest that you go away and live more simply, reduce your consumption, recycle more, think about your carbon footprint and all that. In fact if you are reading this my guess is you are already interested in those things, and they are important. But we have to be careful about merely tending our own garden, because to do so fails to recognise that our garden is really pretty small. We also have a duty to influence others. We have to challenge the world for the sake of the world, something we see Jesus doing at every turn.

So the invitation today is to do something we as Christians seem to dislike heartily: get informed and get political. If you want to see capitalism changed, put into its rightful place as the servant of nature rather than the master of all, and possibly even replaced with another global system altogether, you cannot stand idly by. I work in a shop and am very aware that no one person is consciously seeking to advance the consumerist cause. But collectively every one of us does, and despite all evidence to the contrary very few question that this will deliver the beautiful future we all want.

The seal reminds us that life is more than food and the body more than clothes (Matthew 6:25, Luke 12:23). Relationship, expression, poetry, movement, one-ness with our surroundings, inner peace and alertness – these things are what life is all about. Ask anyone what they want for their life, the answers are the same. Ask people who they admire: it is not the super-rich but those who show a deep humanity and integrity. And yet as a nation we continue to live as if GDP is the only thing that really matters and that every other dream and desire has to be put off until we can afford it – and when will that be?

## Chapter 23

# Red Squirrel – vulnerability, resilience and playful learning

This forest dweller's ancestors were among the first settlers of Britain following the last ice age, unlike other species, such as Rabbits, which were introduced by the Romans and later migrants. Not unlike the earlier British and Celtic peoples, who were forced back by incoming Saxons, the native Reds retreated northwards as the larger Carolina Grey Squirrel, carelessly introduced in the Victorian era for purely aesthetic reasons (yes, some people actually thought the Greys looked nicer), out-competed them for food and passed on a virus against which they still have no defence.

Unlike a lot of our native mammals, Squirrel is active mostly in daylight as indeed are we, so our affinity with her is something to explore. Also like us she does not hibernate in winter but relies on food caches all over the place. If there is a plan to this it is a very obscure one, and it has been noted that she does not always seem to remember where these are, which benefits other animals. Her drey (nest) will be located high up in a tree but is recognisable with a little practice and good pair of binoculars. She is extremely agile, surprisingly robust and constantly alert, which must take a great deal of energy. Generally solitary, she will join others for warmth in winter. Otherwise mating, parenting and fighting over territory will be the only contact she has with others of her kind. This means she needs a relatively large territory. She eats pine nuts and seeds of other trees, fungi, tender shoots and fruit from a variety of plants and will take eggs if the opportunity presents itself.

Grey squirrels are more voracious and general in their eating habits than Reds. Therefore the Red Squirrel is not unlike those human beings who are seeking to live in a more balanced, sustainable way, storing enough to survive but not consuming everything, allowing room for wildness and regeneration. Such people are acutely aware that they are a minority. If you have not experienced it try being vegetarian for a month; cycling instead of driving or giving up reusable plastic bags. You will soon notice that, like those who observe the speed limit on the motorway, the majority seem to be speeding by regardless, unaware that there are millions of us and every single person's lifestyle is having an impact. The Squirrel reminds us to be sensitive, aware of the sacredness, limitations and vulnerability of the 'other' (by which I include elements, land and species, not just other humans).

Finally, like a good many other mammals, Squirrel exhibits a capacity for playfulness, especially when young. This is, of course, valuable in preparing her for adulthood. In the same way that your toddler learns to avoid accidents by climbing all over your furniture, and how to relate to others by fighting over toys and being taught by you (yes, you are having an effect!), Squirrel develops her coordination, strength, intelligence and social skills through play. Like us, she never loses this ability, which can surface at any time, and is especially seen in courtship. "You don't stop playing because you grow old," so the saying goes, "You grow old because you stop playing".

The Grey Squirrel is by far the greatest challenge facing our native Reds. Their introduction was, like so many exotic intro-ductions here and elsewhere, an act of incredible short-sighted ignorance. But what do we do with invasive species now that they are here? Do we simply put up with them, or take some kind of action? Realistically the Grey Squirrel does seem to be here to stay. There are far more of them than us, and any attempt to kill them in high numbers will probably have unintentional effects on other creatures as well. Perhaps the best thing we can do is what we are already doing – protecting certain parts of the country and its surrounding islands from invasion – and make sure we learn from this very sorry lesson.

## From Matthew 17:24-27 (NRSV)

*When they reached Capernaum, the collectors of the temple tax came to Peter and said, "Does your teacher not pay the temple tax?" He said, "Yes, he does." And when he came home, Jesus spoke of it first, asking, "What do you think, Simon? From whom do kings of the earth take toll or tribute? From their children or from others?" When Peter said, "From others," Jesus said to him, "Then the children are free. However, so that we do not give offense to them, go to the sea and cast a hook; take the first fish that comes up; and when you open its mouth, you will find a coin; take that and give it to them for you and me."*

### For reflection and prayer

I have seen books that turn the story about Jesus, Peter and the Temple Tax into yet another miracle, but we are not told that Peter even did what Jesus told him! You may wish to reflect on this. It is just possible Jesus was teasing Peter, who became very defensive of Jesus when challenged. After all, since when did Jesus worry about offending anyone?

How often do you interpret the Bible in a way that suits you, adding to the text where it seems to be lacking? Is Jesus enough for you or do you want to embellish or change him or his words? Does your image of Jesus allow for the possibility that he may have been playful sometimes? Do you find yourself defending Jesus, and can he not look after himself? Can you think of times when Jesus displays agility and perhaps even trespasses where others would prefer to keep him out?

We have far more than five senses, and one of the most important (often taken for granted) is balance. Find a branch you can sit on in a tree, or a stump or some other perch. Remain there for a generous period of time. You may wish to close your eyes for part of this and use your other senses to heighten your awareness of your surroundings. Be aware of your balance, and of your limitations!

# Chapter 24

# Stoat – anger, confrontation and resolution

Unlike many other mammals, Stoat can often be spotted even in the depths of winter if you are prepared to keep still for long enough. Michael Clark[65] writes that they *"seem to have a hypnotic effect on their prey: when pursued, rabbits, for example, appear to become paralysed. Stoats also 'dance' to put birds off their guard, jumping, twisting and rolling ... before suddenly leaping up and rushing* [in]".

Stoat stands for alertness, determination and courage and perhaps impetuousness too, delving into dark places head first and not afraid of conflict. Rabbits, it must be remembered, are quite a bit larger and can fight ferociously when cornered in their own tunnels, which they know intimately. This recklessness is matched by a gift of being able to escape entrapment. If you are a stoat-like person, you will probably have a tendency to act first and apologise later! But the gift of such a personality is playfulness and this is not something to be crushed by those who are more orthodox or conservative.

Like other creatures Stoat's relationship with the earth reminds us that Christ faced, and defeated, evil and did not shy away from personal darkness and death. One online forum post[66] describes it in such a beautiful way I cannot resist quoting verbatim: *"They emerge from burrows like the serpentine energies of spring rising from the winter earth"*. Closely related to weasels and ermines, he has long been considered mystical, moving between different worlds, owing to his ease of movement from one environment to another and the way his coat changes colour in winter, enabling him to disappear in the snow.

Christ, like the Stoat, also warns and brings judgement, but his words are always for our good and not our destruction. In his

apparent harshness towards those who sought a rigorous spirituality, Jesus was offering an invitation not condemnation, and a
reminder that it is possible to intervene inappropriately in other
peoples' lives and so trespass on holy ground.

Habitat loss is the biggest challenge for them at present and
has been for some time. Encourage landowners to consider
making room for grassland, heaths and woods and find out what
your local Wildlife Trust is doing.

## From Matthew 23:1-15 (NRSV)

*Then Jesus said to the crowds and to his disciples, "The scribes and
the Pharisees sit on Moses' seat; therefore, do whatever they teach
you and follow it; but do not do as they do, for they do not practice
what they teach. They tie up heavy burdens, hard to bear, and lay
them on the shoulders of others; but they themselves are unwilling
to lift a finger to move them ... woe to you, scribes and Pharisees,
hypocrites! For you lock people out of the kingdom of heaven. For
you do not go in yourselves, and when others are going in, you stop
them. Woe to you, scribes and Pharisees, hypocrites! For you cross
sea and land to make a single convert, and you make the new convert
twice as much a child of hell as yourselves...."*

## For reflection and prayer

Jesus took on the Pharisees, especially those who had control of
the Temple in Jerusalem, knowing that it would lead to his death.
Even so, there were some among that group who were able to see
beyond their own limits. If you are a bit of a stoat yourself, how
do you experience your confrontations with others? Have you
sometimes failed to heed your own warnings and rushed in too
blindly? If you are not this type of person, how do you react to
them? Are you able to value someone who is so different,
unorthodox and challenging? How can our worshipping communities celebrate the particular gifts that such people bring, recog-

nising them as another aspect of the body of Christ? How do I feel about Jesus when I hear him ranting in this way?

Many people like the story of Jesus overturning the money tables (Matthew 21:12, John 2:15), but we are less comfortable with our own anger. The task today is to find a way to express your anger to God, perhaps by hurling a stone into the sea (don't choose one that is too small or easy to hurl) or, if you are inland, by driving a stick into the ground. You may need more than one stone or stick. As you do this, let the action and its outcomes speak to you. If necessary, confide in a trusted friend (you may ask them to come with you as a prayerful witness if that would help) and write about the experience in your journal. If you are angry with God – and many people are – then direct the stone or the stick or whatever at God, not anyone else, expressing yourself in words too if you can, and mark how God receives this.

## Chapter 25

# Common Toad – born of the Spirit

There is a species of Toad – the Natterjack – that seems to have been endangered for most of my lifetime. This is his better known... I was going to say *cousin*, but that would be lazy thinking. They are separate species and in fact where they occur together the tadpoles of the Common Toad will eat those of the Natterjack. This book *is* concerned with conservation, but as part of a bigger picture of communion, so I am not focussing specifically on endangered species. Apart from anything else that would play into the hands of one of our prejudices: that something is more important because it is rare. If you ever find yourself saying, as I have, something along the lines of "Ooh what's that? Oh, it's only a wood pigeon" then you are familiar enough with this way of thinking, which may have more to do with market capitalism than any true sense of worth. Too many of our indigenous creatures are named with this "common" prefix, which feeds this laziness. It is something to pray about. But today's subject is the Common Toad, and some of what is true for her will also be seen in other Toad species. She is, perhaps naturally enough, often confused with Frog, another non-cousin, whom we considered in chapter 11.

You can tell it is her in a number of ways: she walks rather than hops, her body is broad, she has lumps on her skin (usually referred to as "warts", although I have not found anything to indicate these are caused by a virus, such as those people get on their hands or feet) and she stays away from water except for when she mates. This is one of the first things she does upon waking from the long sleep of winter, heading for the same pond, lake or slow stretch of river each year. The male grasps her from behind – he is smaller than she and may even get into position while she is still on the way – and remains there for a few days, fertilising her eggs as she lays them. It is one of the easiest times to spot her. Do not be fooled by any croaking though: that will almost certainly be a male telling another male that he has made a mistake! Toadspawn takes the form of long strings, rather than the amorphous mass laid by frogs. The Tadpoles (Toadpoles?) hatch about ten days later and turn into tiny little Toadlets within two months. Throughout July these will start climbing out to look for food and a place to spend the winter, and so the cycle continues.

Although Toad copes well with dry places she still needs some dampness to keep her skin in good condition and for this reason is more likely to be seen after rain. Her base of operations is a burrow which she digs out herself and in the winter, if this is not deep enough, she buries herself in leaf litter or under a fallen log to hibernate from November through to March. A night prowler, she feeds on insects and their larvae, spiders, worms and slugs. She may even take a Harvest Mouse if she is big enough. Her method is to remain utterly still, waiting for prey to pass by and then she moves with frightening rapidity. Her natural life, if she avoids predators, sickness and accident, is around forty years. She greatly improves her chances by secreting an irritating substance from glands just behind her eyes, although this does not seem to affect Hedgehogs or Grass Snakes. Her skin colour generally matches that of the soil where she lives, so there is some variation in different areas. If she feels threatened she will puff herself up and may stand on her hind legs to look as big as possible.

I was interested to find out that the pagan websites I checked all seem to put Toad and Frog together, sometimes even treating them as one animal. One of them, which will be nameless, got a few facts completely wrong and in general I felt that the links with what might be called "spiritual realities" were rather tenuous. The one thing that does ring true is that they embody transformation, especially early in life. For us too, the first stages are significantly formative. Many of us still carry vivid memories from early life, and there are powerful messages we may have internalised even before we had the capacity to consciously remember. But how can we apply this to our adulthood?

There are some creatures for whom "common" belies the true state of the population, but at present she is not one of those. You can find her pretty much anywhere on the British mainland. There has been some decline in populations, however, and apart from being driven over as they cross roads to get to breeding sites, the other problem is the disappearance of ponds in general. I know people are wary of ponds (we certainly are) because of cases where children have tragically drowned, but if you can have a pond in your garden it will benefit wildlife and, with reasonable security, can provide an amazing wonderland for children, accompanied by adults, to discover a huge amount at firsthand.

## From Matthew 18:1-5 (NRSV)

*At that time the disciples came to Jesus and asked, "Who is the greatest in the kingdom of heaven?" He called a child, whom he put among them, and said, "Truly I tell you, unless you change and become like children, you will never enter the kingdom of heaven. Whoever becomes humble like this child is the greatest in the kingdom of heaven. Whoever welcomes one such child in my name welcomes me."*

## For reflection and prayer

Jesus' words to his disciples about becoming like a child are consistent with his conversation with Nicodemus in John chapter 3. There he goes even further, saying we need to be "born again". It is a powerful concept, although we need to overcome the rather cheesy overtones it may have for us in a culture that has become fashionably cynical about faith. Transformation is not something we can do ourselves, just as the Tadpole does not choose to become a Toadlet and then an adult. It is a natural process. But there may be times in life when we have to make decisions that follow the flow of what God is doing. I had this experience myself when I took a big decision to step away from full time Anglican ministry. There was, and is, a strange combination of excitement and vulnerability, of venturing into unknown territory, and even though I have not yet met anyone who thinks I did the wrong thing, I still have days when I look back. Jesus spoke about that too (Luke 9:62), and I often have to remind myself of his mercy.

In fact, if we allow it, transformation happens to us all the time. At a physical level we regularly vacuum up the results of bodies that are in a constantly dynamic state of renewal. "You learn something new every day" is a common enough comment, and as we get older I firmly believe our capacity for wonder increases. In that same conversation with Nicodemus Jesus said; "The wind blows where it chooses, and you hear the sound of it, but you do not know where it comes from or where it goes. *So it is with everyone who is born of the Spirit*" (my emphasis). So we can expect followers of Christ to be unpredictable, even to themselves.

Every stage of life involves integrating something from past stages and preparing for future stages. To do this is not a failure to live in the present. As adults we are wonderfully equipped to do important inner work that we could not do before. When we reach older adulthood we have work we could not do in middle age and so on. If you could characterise your life at the moment as a season, what would it be? What is there that you need to let go of in order to take hold of what is now? What do you have now that, although valuable, will not be yours forever? Take some time to speak about these things to God, or to write them in your journal. It may be that some other means of expression (painting, music composition, dance, poetry) occurs to you. Trust your instinct and let the Spirit within you blow where she chooses.

# Chapter 26

# Trees – wise guardians of time

I know we have already considered the Ash but before we look at any more trees I want to say something more general about them. This is because as a phenomenon they are unlike anything else you will find in this book.

It was at the Greenbelt Festival in 2014 that I first tried something like Tai Chi. As a volunteer at The Grove venue, I saw a good many groups come and do their thing and, when I wasn't welcoming those who turned up, I was able to do a lot of participating. One of the contributors led us in some simple exercises that involved slow movement of the body in time with our breathing. I found it to be very stilling and peaceful and decided to take some of the exercises into my own prayer practice.

Near where I live, and on my way to work, are a couple of relatively small public spaces and, because I start work horribly early, I can easily find an outdoor space to myself for ten minutes on my way there. It is in these parks that I have encountered certain trees, but the cool half light of the early hour has meant that identification is difficult. The advantage of this is that I have been able to meet these mysterious creatures as they are, without any preconceived idea of what I will find, allowing their stillness to speak to me in the short time I have with them each morning.

In 1985 the composer John Cage wrote a piece entitled "ASLSP 1985", which he adapted for organ two years later. The letters stand for "As SLow aS Possible" [sic], a title which has led to a few renditions by individual organists of herculean length. Then, in September 2001, a performance of the piece began in St. Burchardi church in Halberstadt, Germany which is intended to last for over six centuries. If I understand the website[67] correctly, an apple tree was planted at the same time. Both the music and the tree are "symbols of confidence in the future". So this musical creation quite intentionally resonates with the life of trees, a song whose rhythms and changes span centuries.

For many the words "Sing a new song to the Lord" (Psalm 96) have been an instruction to continually refresh the hymn book. That is certainly one way to read it, but for me this verse has another interpretation. I do not believe we are made for a purpose, like tools in a toolbox or machine parts in a grand design. My own experience and belief is that we are more like works of art – paintings, dance, drama, music – that express the likeness of the creator. So for me the psalm is an invitation to make my life a "new song to the Lord". In those early mornings I find myself praying in the company of long-lived and mysterious giants who were here long before me. The sense I get from them is that they are fully present, but they also hold a far greater vision, a longer span of time, than I am used to considering. Their size and their longevity gives me a sense of how young and inexperienced I am, and whenever I am with them I sense I am being observed in much the same way as a very gentle and wise old person might observe a child. "Who is this?" they seem to say, not to me but to each other, and with all the guilessness of a toddler learning to speak I say "I am a child of earth". I also had, one morning, a profound sense in my workplace of the forest that once stood there and with it came the realisation that a forest may well one day return. So may I encourage you to encounter the trees in your neighbourhood and elsewhere before you identify them? Spend time in the presence of these creatures who, unlike the animals, fungi and other plant-life in this book will almost certainly outlive you. Let time pass and do not be in too great a hurry. Receive what they have to give you and remember that they have been created by the same power that gives you life and breath. They are not here by accident, and they have much to impart.

116

## Chapter 27

# Hawthorn – suffering and endurance

We planted a Hawthorn hedge in February 2009 at the last house
we lived in. It was the year we got married and so perhaps that
is why he has become so special to me. He has many names:
Hawthorn comes from the Saxon word for hedge ("Haga");
"Quickthorn" – because the cuttings were "quick" (old English
for alive) and could be planted straight into the ground; May
(after the month, not the other way around), Whitethorn,
Hawberry, Thornberry and even "Bread and Cheese". The story
I heard is that children would eat the leaves and suck the flesh
from the haw berries as a snack before heading home for their
tea, although it has also been suggested people turned to it in
times of austerity. I cannot say I have got much out of the
experience, but give it a try. If nothing else it is an unusual thing
to eat and helps break a kind of taboo we often
have about the perils of wild food. By the same
token you can also try making Hawthorn
schnapps, steeping the haws in vodka (the same
process as sloe gin). Although most commonly
used in hedging (a tradition that is being
revived at the present time) if allowed to grow
he can become a tall tree, up to 15m. He occurs
all over Europe in most soil types, is hermaphrodite (both male and female in each individual
plant) and features in a great deal of folklore
and mythology. He is one of the "Ogham[68]
trees" and is also associated with the ancient runic letter
Thurisaz (pronounced "th" and called thorn).

"It [sic] is the food plant for caterpillars of many moths,
including the hawthorn, orchard ermine, pear leaf blister,

rhomboid tortrix, light emerald, lackey, vapourer, fruitlet mining tortrix, small eggar and lappet moths. Its [sic] flowers are eaten by dormice and provide nectar and pollen for bees and other pollinating insects. The haws are rich in antioxidants and are eaten by many migrating birds such as redwings, fieldfares and thrushes, as well as small mammals".

In fact over three hundred different insect species[69] are supported by him; his wood is hard and good for carving, tools and other uses that require resilience; and it burns extremely well. And yet Hawthorn has long been considered an unlucky plant, whose flowers smell of death (owing to the presence of trimethylamine, which is also released when flesh begins to decompose), the "Thorn", or "Thurisaz", rune stands for a blade or a serpent's bite. His impenetrable nature evokes awareness of limitations, personal risk, and the possibility of being trapped or stabbed in the back.[70] As Christians we are, of course, aware of the part thorns play in the story of Christ's betrayal, entrapment and suffering. For me, however, few trees seem to reflect the passing seasons as well as Hawthorn and for this reason I believe he stands for something intensely positive. It is believed that it was a Hawthorn around which people used to dance in May, leading to the maypole tradition. Garlands would be worn, made of "knots" of Hawthorn blossom, which later morphed into the song "here we go gathering nuts [knots] in may". The saying "ne'er cast a clout 'til May be out" refers not to the month but to the May (Hawthorn) blossom. He is among the first to flower in spring, his fruit lasts through the late summer period into the start of winter and even denuded of his leaves he remains formidable, unconquerable, while the freezing winds whip and whistle through his unflinching boughs.

## From Mark 9:14-29 (NRSV)

*When they came to the disciples, they saw a great crowd around them, and some scribes arguing with them.... He asked them, "What are you arguing about with them?" Someone from the crowd answered him, "Teacher, I brought you my son; he has a spirit that makes him unable to speak; and whenever it seizes him, it dashes him down; and he foams and grinds his teeth and becomes rigid; and I asked your disciples to cast it out, but they could not do so." He answered them, "You faithless generation, how much longer must I be among you? How much longer must I put up with you? Bring him to me." And they brought the boy to him. When the spirit saw him, immediately it convulsed the boy, and he fell on the ground and rolled about, foaming at the mouth. Jesus asked the father, "How long has this been happening to him?" And he said, "From childhood. It has often cast him into the fire and into the water, to destroy him; but if you are able to do anything, have pity on us and help us." Jesus said to him, "If you are able! —All things can be done for the one who believes." Immediately the father of the child cried out, "I believe; help my unbelief!" When Jesus saw that a crowd came running together, he rebuked the unclean spirit, saying to it, "You spirit that keeps this boy from speaking and hearing, I command you, come out of him, and never enter him again!" After crying out and convulsing him terribly, it came out, and the boy was like a corpse, so that most of them said, "He is dead." But Jesus took him by the hand and lifted him up, and he was able to stand. When he had entered the house, his disciples asked him privately, "Why could we not cast it out?" He said to them, "This kind can come out only through prayer."*

## For reflection and prayer

One of the more tragic sights in the countryside is a hawthorn hedge that has been flailed. This may be the quickest and cheapest way to deal with the new growth but over time it destroys this icon of our countryside, giving a hedge full of ugly holes in the short term. Traditional hedge-laying, by contrast, results in a thick and impenetrable tangle, one of Britain's classic habitats. So perhaps one lesson from the Hawthorn is that worthwhile and lasting outcomes are rarely achieved quickly, easily or cheaply. In the same way we see Jesus pressing on through what seems like impenetrable barriers of human obstinacy and doubt. His answer to the difficulty the disciples had in casting out the demon reminds us that the things that count usually require work, loving and effortful attention (some of the early sources say "prayer and fasting", which underlines this point). How does a culture so obsessed with convenience recover this sense and create things that are lasting and worthwhile? How can I do that at an individual level, and explore it with others?

# Chapter 28

# Hedgehog – being known and being loved

I quite like the old West Country name, "Furze-pig", although she is not very closely related to pigs, despite the grunting. This is another creature that enjoys a lot of attention, with whole websites dedicated to fascinating facts, and yet as we shall see she is a real stranger to us. I heartily recommend Hugh Warwick's book, *A Prickly Affair*,[71] if you are looking for something to take you a bit deeper.

Her body has a combination of hair types, including the iconic spines (Hedgehogs are the only spiny British mammal), of which there are an estimated five thousand on each adult,[72] and the thick, soft, warm fur of her belly. When threatened she famously curls into a tight ball, the spines looking like a miniature version of the pikes at an historic battle recreation. It is an effective defence against most predators and she needs it because these include foxes and badgers as well as the now absent wolves and bears that used to roam the woods. She is a predator too, living on all kinds of invertebrates, Frogs, Toads (despite the noxious substance these secrete onto their bodies) and the eggs of ground-nesting birds. Some of her kind have even been known to take snakes, although I am not sure how common that is, and males will occasionally eat baby hedgehogs if the mother is not aggressive enough to stop them (see "lessons from nature" below).

Very much a nighttime prowler, she has poor eyesight and so relies upon other senses. She hides during the day in nests on the ground, working her way under thick brush or anything that provides cover (perhaps most notoriously those piles of sticks that provide such wonderful comfort to us on Bonfire Night). Like most wild animals she can play host to fleas and other parasites (although it is not clear how prevalent that is). There is one species of flea that lives nowhere else.

Hedgehogs are real loners. They only come together to mate and when that is accomplished – usually with a great deal of noise after courtship, which can go on for hours – the male heads off into the (metaphorical) sunset. Those young who survive (she usually gives birth to up to a dozen pups, also called "kits" or "urchins") will leave the mother within eight weeks of birth. She hibernates in winter, allowing her body temperature to drop and her heart rate slows to just one beat per minute. This requires considerable preparatory feasting in the autumn. And if all that is not strange enough, she "anoints" herself with saliva for reasons no one has yet been able to fathom.

The Hedgehog, then, is yet another paradox: a commonplace stranger. Her habits are the very opposite of ours. She is yet another reminder that the world is not here just for our convenience. She is the neighbour who must be loved (Mark 12:28-31), the stranger who is to be welcomed (Hebrews 13:2). She is certainly not our enemy. This needs to be said because although we rarely target her with direct aggression, she suffers considerable collateral damage from our attacks on other species and our lifestyle choices (one online forum post cites rat poison, slug pellets, pesticides, strimmers, intensive farming and fencing with concrete footings). One solution requires coordinated community action: as many of us as possible need to make small holes in the bottoms of our garden fences. This allows them to establish territories and encounter one another. The plus side for us is the slugs she will consume free of charge, not to mention the pleasure of seeing her making her way through. With rapid decline in the Hedgehog population, from an estimated 30 million in the 1950s to fewer than one million today,[73] we cannot afford to be complacent.

So the hedgehog reminds us, as so many species in this book will, that even the most familiar things can be essentially "other" and should be respected. She is a living reminder not to rush to judgment but to spend time in contemplation, recognising that we often scratch only the surface of things.

## From Luke 19:1-10 (NRSV)

*He entered Jericho and was passing through it. A man was there named Zacchaeus; he was a chief tax collector and was rich. He was trying to see who Jesus was, but on account of the crowd he could not, because he was short in stature. So he ran ahead and climbed a sycamore tree to see him, because he was going to pass that way. When Jesus came to the place, he looked up and said to him, "Zacchaeus, hurry and come down; for I must stay at your house today." So he hurried down and was happy to welcome him. All who saw it began to grumble and said, "He has gone to be the guest of one who is a sinner." Zacchaeus stood there and said to the Lord, "Look, half of my possessions, Lord, I will give to the poor; and if I have defrauded anyone of anything, I will pay back four times as much." Then Jesus said to him, "Today salvation has come to this house, because he too is a son of Abraham. For the Son of Man came to seek out and to save the lost."*

## Lessons from nature

There are times when people attempt to resolve arguments by citing an example in nature, or by claiming that a certain practice or product is "natural". Hedgehogs teach us that such "lessons" are pretty spurious and not to be trusted. Nature produces hurricanes as well as gentle breezes, floods as well as trickling streams, sharp spines as well as soft fur. This is not easy for Christians to assimilate, because we want to find grace in nature not simply the law of tooth and claw, but God is not an idea, and does not exist in some imaginary realm. God is indeed found only in reality or, as the Ignatian author Gerard Hughes[74] puts it "God is in the facts".

## For reflection and Prayer

The facts about Zacchaeus are sparse in Luke's account. His shortness is probably the least important thing about him; it is not really relevant that he climbed a tree. But preachers and teachers the world over like to fill in the blanks. I was told as a child that he was hiding from Jesus as well as trying to see him, that tax collectors always cheated people, that he had a low self-esteem. None of these are in the text. I would also like to suggest that his offer to pay back four times anyone he has defrauded could be read as a statement of innocence, not guilt. Could it be that in his case we need to look beneath the surface, as Jesus did, to find God in the facts rather than in the traditional stereotype? Could it be that there are Zacchaeuses near to us who also need to be looked upon with respect as those to be with, even to eat with, rather than avoided?

Collect six sticks of roughly equal length and use nettle rope or string to bind them into a classic "window frame" shape. Use this as a reminder that there are four parts to you and to every other creature. This model is called the "Johari Window" and is set out below.

| Known Self:<br><br>what we know about ourselves and others know about us | Known Self:<br><br>what we know about ourselves and others do not know |
|---|---|
| Unknown self:<br><br>what others know about us that we do not know | Unknown self:<br><br>what neither we nor others know about us |

As far as I know this is not a specifically Christian model but for me it chimes very well with the way of Jesus. Spend some time contemplating how knowledge of yourself can move from one "pane" to another as you grow and how, in later life, it can pass back out of your ability to hold it. There is a real compassion here, because God sees it all and loves it all. Nothing is lost, our true life is "hidden with Christ in God" (Colossians 3:3) and there is potential for the light of Christ to shine through the whole of us, not just the bits we choose to show to the world. The hedgehog may be unapologetic, perhaps even a bit boorish (boarish?) but she is known and loved, and so are you.

# Chapter 29

# Jay – mindfulness and symbiosis

On the day that I completed the chapter on Magpie my wife and son saw a Jay. They told me about it just as I was going into the Library to write. So with Magpie metaphorically in the bag, I sat back and glanced around, wondering which creature would come next. Immediately my eye lighted on a book called *Wild*. Looking more closely I saw that the author was someone called Jay![75] My plan had been to write about Deer or Stag, and no doubt I will, but clearly the Corvids are still calling for my attention, so here we go.

Here is a real contradiction: an incredibly shy bird that is also one of the largest and most brightly coloured on these islands, whose piercing shriek earns them the Gaelic nickname 'schreachag choille' – literally 'woodland screamer'.[76] They are spread right across the country (except northern Scotland) but unlike other crows, Jays stick to woodlands (deciduous and coniferous) and although my interest for this book is in native British species it is worth noting that they are also found right across North Africa, Europe and Asia. His chief food is acorns, which like the Squirrel he stores when in good supply, and other nuts, seeds, insects and – yes he is a Corvid alright – eggs, nestlings and small mammals. This burying of acorns helps Oak to spread. He also allows ants to swarm across his body, which helps rid him of other insects. So one of the key words for Jay is "symbiosis".

I tend to flinch inwardly these days when an animal is described as "intelligent" because this is always taken from a human perspective. It is tempting to ask who we are to set the standard since, with all our knowledge, we are still managing to wreck the planet. But Jay has been known to fix his gaze on another creature and watch,[77] learning from observation, picking up the clues he needs to fulfil his own particular goal. This behaviour is unusual (or maybe we just haven't seen it much) and gives an indication of what Jay may have to share with us, if we are willing to pay attention.

## From Mark 12:41-44 (NRSV)

*He sat down opposite the treasury, and watched the crowd putting money into the treasury. Many rich people put in large sums. A poor widow came and put in two small copper coins, which are worth a penny. Then he called his disciples and said to them, "Truly I tell you, this poor widow has put in more than all those who are contributing to the treasury. For all of them have contributed out of their abundance; but she out of her poverty has put in everything she had, all she had to live on."*

## For reflection and prayer

In this reading Jesus pays close attention to something and encourages his disciples to do the same. This ability to be attentive, sometimes in the midst of great distraction, is one of his great qualities. It enables him to focus on what is essential and let other things pass. Later on (John 12:20-32) he is approached by some people, via Philip, who want to see him but instead of responding to the request he acts as if he has not even heard it. This is a reminder that Jesus has his own agenda, his own self-understanding, and is not there to be everything we want him to be. This story appears also in Luke's account (chapter 21), which of all the Gospels most emphasises the place of prayer in Jesus' life. Can we also develop a prayer life that enables us to be more attentive and focussed in the situations we face each day?

# Chapter 30

# Mole – the power of solitude and reticence

Tunnelling is what makes Mole both famous and infamous: up to 20 metres per day and producing numerous instantly recognisable mounds.[78] The earth from these is excellent for potting plants and her work aerates the soil, but it is rare to find a gardener who welcomes her. We were there when she first arrived in the garden of our last house and, five years on, she has outlasted us. Those tunnels just under the surface are a simple but elegant system of food capture, as the creatures Mole eats (mostly earthworms but supplemented with pretty much any invertebrate she comes across, and even snakes and lizards) simply fall in. Further down there will be a large nesting chamber lined with dry grass and at least one food store stocked with beheaded earthworms. I have no idea how she copes with flooding. Does anyone?

Her underground habit has resulted in vestigial eyes that are almost completely obscured by fur, ears that similarly cannot be clearly seen and a very well developed nose with highly sensitive whiskers. Her front paws have developed into broad, outwardly-turned clawed shovels. Deep soil is pretty much the only requirement for her and apart from gardens she is found in farmland, grassland and woods. Moles occur right across Northern Europe but not, surprisingly, in Ireland. She (thinking specifically about females) has a feature unique among mammals, called *ovotestes*, which seem to have both an ovary *and* a testicle. The resulting testosterone is thought to account for the similarities between the sexes, including comparable levels of aggression.

If you think Hedgehog is antisocial you need to spend some time contemplating Mole! She will staunchly defend her territory against all other moles. Mating happens in spring with a male tunnelling into her space, mating and then departing immediately. The only litter of the short breeding season, between two to seven pups, will themselves scatter around 33 days after they are born, travelling above ground, when they are often picked off by other predators. Look around where you see molehills and you may spot the entrance hole, which will not have a mound of earth.

It is something of an understatement to say we are, as a species, far more communal than moles. We are, in fact, super-cooperators,[79] able to harness the energies of a diverse group as long as there is a shared vision. So what can we gather from this strangely introverted neighbour? Perhaps a recovery of the "power of alone", to borrow a phrase from Simon Parke?[80] Because as much as we are drawn to, and need, community, we are also inherently autonomous. The early Church was never fully assimilated into the state, even when it became the official religion,[81] because its members were fiercely independent as well as united around their common belief. There is a balancing act here:

> Let him [sic] who cannot be alone beware of community ... Let him [sic] who is not in community beware of being alone ... Each by itself has profound perils and pitfalls. One who wants fellowship without solitude plunges into the void of words and feelings, and the one who seeks solitude without fellowship perishes in the abyss of vanity, self-infatuation and despair.

...writes Dietrich Bonhoeffer.[82] For each of us the balance will be different. Some need more solitary time; some get more than they need. It is probably rare to get it just right.

Common and not protected, she is persecuted by anyone who wants to establish their "right" to land which was there before them and will be there after them. I would argue that the "damage" she supposedly does is mostly cosmetic and has little real cost impact. So why not welcome these creatures, who are demonstrating the health and biodiversity of your soil by their presence? If you do so your action, which may not seem like much, will be a radical protest against an attitude that has for too long been prevalent among humans. The earth is not ours (Psalm 24:1), and some who have a closer connection to it should be given room.

### From Luke 6:12-16, 20 (NRSV)

*Now during those days he went out to the mountain to pray; and he spent the night in prayer to God. And when day came, he called his disciples and chose twelve of them, whom he also named apostles:*

*Simon, whom he named Peter, and his brother*
*Andrew, and*
*James, and*
*John, and*
*Philip, and*
*Bartholomew, and*
*Matthew, and*
*Thomas, and*
*James son of Alphaeus, and*
*Simon, who was called the Zealot, and*
*Judas son of James, and*
*Judas Iscariot, who became a traitor.*

*...Then he looked up at his disciples and said; "Blessed are you who are poor, for yours is the kingdom of God...."*

### For reflection and prayer
Jesus seemed on purpose to call together a pretty dysfunctional

community. They certainly had differing values, and we know they spent more time than was either healthy or necessary discussing what the order of precedent should be among them (Matthew 18:1, Luke 9:46, Luke 22:24). Somehow they finally managed to work out that "hierarchy" is not really part of God's way of working. They also seem to have failed to pass that deep knowledge on to many of the institutions that today call themselves "the Church". Is this because, in the normal human dynamic we are not spending enough time in solitary prayer? One of the challenges of nature connection is getting beyond this tendency to look always to our human group, and yet I firmly believe we are called *together*, not just individually, to explore nature connection. Perhaps the reserve, even the aggression, of Mole has a place here. We should not too easily enter other people's space, or expect them to come into ours. Generally extraverted, I share with intraverted[83] friends a struggle with that part of the communion service called "the peace" (apologies to non-Anglicans at this point – perhaps you have your own irritants instead). I do not want to be told how to interact with others in such a controlled, prescribed, way (although even that is not as bad as the ordination service I once attended where the booklet included the words "The new clergy leave to the sponta-neous applause of the congregation"!). But it is not really aggressive to hold back a bit. It is about choosing what to share and when, and it means that anything that is shared is a true gift.

One of the great surprises of solitary prayer is that it actually draws us into closer fellowship with others. I experienced this myself in the mid-1990s when, working at Lee Abbey in North Devon, I found a rare peace that brought with it a genuine heart for others. In particular I remember feeling an incredible and inexplicable closeness to the people of Haiti, a country I have never been to and know very little about. I have heard something similar about Thomas Merton's experience of solitary prayer during the conflict in Vietnam.[84] In the same way, perhaps Mole is closer to the communion of nature than we realise. Her life, in contact with the raw, damp earth, may give her a deeper knowing than we are accustomed to inhabiting. Is this knowing available to us? We will only find it if we look. So spend some time alone with the earth. Place your hands upon it and look at it. Extend your awareness downwards and listen. Take time over this and follow your instincts. This practice is a normal part of the services led by Ancient Arden Forest Church, something they have kindly shared with other Forest Church groups.[85] It requires a certain maturity because it is easy to feel self-conscious. An incredibly simple, even obvious, action, but how many of us have even thought of it?

## Chapter 31

# Kingfisher – setting our eyes upon the goal

What must it be like to make yourself a dart, plunging with the force of earth's gravity, upon a single silvery point in the water below? For an instant you are poised, hanging in air, weightless, and time stands still. Then, with a gathering rush of wind, it is though the world suddenly collapses, contracted in, every muscle held tight as the drop begins. In split seconds you have reached an unimaginable speed, the surface rushes up to meet you, your eyes close involuntarily in the last moments, your beak grasps flesh, wings fling outwards, you bounce in the water's firm hold, brought to the surface by the recoil. It is finished.

You will have experienced, no doubt, in a crowded room the phenomenon of following a conversation nearby that you are not involved in, to the cost of the one you are. Or perhaps you have failed to hear a person in the same room speaking directly to you because the radio or TV in the corner is being more interesting or insistent in that moment. Both of these examples relate to hearing, but we can do this with sight as well. We are attuned to spotting the things that are relevant to us, even out of the corner of our eyes and this we share with the Kingfisher. He knows the river intimately, where the strategic perches are, and moves from one to another, aware of the predators' approach. Even when scanning the gentle water below for his own prey, he is alert to the recognisable, though subtle, movement at the edge of vision, the shadow that betrays his oncoming enemy. Notoriously hard to spot and intensely shy, he is often no more than a blue flash across our vision, hardly visible despite his striking plumage. His nest too is subtle: a hole in a vertical river bank no more than half a metre above the water line and barely larger than his diminutive body. This will be the entrance to a tunnel that may be nearly one metre long, with a single chamber at the end whose slight depression will stop his eggs from rolling out. Inside there is nothing but bare earth. This means at one level he might represent the link between three worlds – earth, air and water – and the relationship between them. But this nest and the way he lives means he also represents poverty, as we shall see in a moment.

He depends upon relatively still, or gently flowing, water for his food (sticklebacks, minnows and other small fish, insects, shrimps and tadpoles). He is young, breeding in his first year and producing with his mate up to three clutches of eggs (six or seven at a time), usually in the same nest, from the end of March. Both parents incubate the eggs and feed the chicks in turn. Once a chick has fed she goes to the back of the burrow and waits for her siblings. The chicks leave the nest in just over three weeks and are fed for only a few days more before the parents drive them off to manage for themselves. The mortality rate is high, as many young have not learned to fish before they are sent away. Only one quarter survive to breed, and only one quarter of adults live more than a year. Their small size makes them vulnerable throughout the winter months (which rather gives the lie to one website's description of them as a symbol of abundance and prosperity). Their beauty and skill reminds us that looks can be deceptive and that the glory of God is often seen not in the strong of the world but in weakness, vulnerability and dependence (1 Corinthians 1:27-28). And he is intensely vulnerable. A severe winter can cut a swathe through Kingfisher populations that take years to recover, as can a poor summer. Really his only defence is to produce as many young as possible. But in that magical moment when he surges towards his prey, then his true quality is seen.

We need to protect river banks and trees that overhang the stiller stretches of rivers and canals. Please make sure any cat you own is well fed and clumsy (they are the main killers of

Kingfishers, with rats coming a close second) and consider not keeping a cat in future. I realise this is controversial, but domestic cats are not native to Britain and cause such a huge amount of harm; I believe it is irresponsible not to at least consider reducing their numbers. By far the best way to do that is not to buy one in the first place (see final chapter). Organic farming methods and protecting rivers from pollution will also increase the number of suitable habitats.

Kingfisher is rare and easily disturbed. He will not enter his nest if he feels threatened. The chicks need to eat plenty of fish so if they are left for too long they will stop calling and the parents will therefore stop feeding them. So if you spot a nest, take note and move quickly on, as tempting as it is (and it is) to stay and see them come and go.

Thankfully the law gives Kingfisher the highest level of protection (Schedule 1 of the Wildlife and Countryside Act 1981). Disturbing them in the breeding season, deliberately or otherwise, carries a heavy fine and it is illegal to photograph them without a licence. So find out where they are and please steer clear.

## From Luke 9:51-53, 57 and 13:31-34 (NRSV)

*When the days drew near for him to be taken up, he set his face to go to Jerusalem. And he sent messengers ahead of him. On their way they entered a village of the Samaritans to make ready for him; but they did not receive him, because his face was set toward Jerusalem....*

*As they were going along the road, someone said to him, "I will follow you wherever you go." And Jesus said to him, "Foxes have holes, and birds of the air have nests; but the Son of Man has nowhere to lay his head."...*

*At that very hour some Pharisees came and said to him, "Get away from here, for Herod wants to kill you." He said to them, "Go and tell that fox for me, 'Listen, I am casting out demons and performing cures today and tomorrow, and on the third day I finish my work. Yet today, tomorrow, and the next day I must be on my way, because it is impossible for a prophet to be killed outside of Jerusalem.' Jerusalem, Jerusalem, the city that kills the prophets and stones those who are sent to it! How often have I desired to gather your children together as a hen gathers her brood under her wings, and you were not willing!"*

## For reflection and prayer

For Jesus the third day has become the focus, the goal (we will see this elsewhere too). He turns himself to face it. An arrow nocked, his eyes turn to Jerusalem. This has always been the target. Now it is in sight. He is taking aim, closing in upon that moment of completion when it will be accomplished, bursting through the surface of death, grasping and destroying utterly the destructive evil that lies beneath death's shimmering surface, spreading his arms to be caught by the Spirit's receiving embrace, and rising again. This moment, enacted at the outset, in the arms of the Baptizer John (Luke 3:21-22), now to be brought to completion, fulfilment, in the fire of the cross (Luke 12:50). How does this image change the way you understand Jesus, who was also young and poor, whose high-risk strategy was to create as many children of faith as possible, "born, not of blood or of the will of the flesh or of the will of man, but of God" (John 1:13, NRSV) and who calls us to follow him in the way of vulnerability and trust? It is he who spots us, shimmering beneath the surface of our own self-deceit, and he closes in, intent upon our rebirth.

## Chapter 32

# Mayfly – celebrating all we have

Rules are not there simply to be obeyed, or just to be broken for that matter. They are in place to facilitate something. Some of the most impressive art arises because of some restriction placed on the artist, and some of the most interesting innovation can come about when the artist pushes the boundaries of a form. Anyway, all this is my excuse for choosing, with this family of creatures, to cite their "scientific" name on this occasion, the "Ephemeroptera" (first given by Aristotle, of all people). There are over two thousand individual species of Mayfly in the world, all with an incredibly short lifespan (by human reckoning) in common. They are one of the most ubiquitous insects on earth, existing virtually everywhere except the two polar environments and some remote islands. Britain has upwards of forty-five different species, also called "upwinged" flies, owing to their habit of holding their wings in an upright position at rest. For fairly obvious, narcissistic, reasons I could not resist *Ephemera danica*, which also happens to be the best known species in this country, probably because it is the largest, and is therefore the one that everyone here calls a Mayfly (although the Natural History Museum also lists the names Green Drake, Black Drake, Grey Drake and Green Dun).[86]

Being an older dad (our children were born when I was 42 and 45) I feel I have good reason to be glad that we live somewhat longer than Mayflies, some of whom exist as mature insects for less than one hour. Our gift is that we have a long life, giving time for reflection and exploration, growth and community. Yes, there are many aspects to the life we have. There is a beautiful book, ostensibly for children (but the best in that genre always have something to say to those in different stages of life as well) by

Jeanne Willis called *Mayfly Day*[87] which calls into question our natural reaction, that it is sad to live such a short time,[88] and challenges us to live as fully and intentionally as this extraordinary creature. Of course this book does something that I normally struggle with (back to rules again!) in that it projects human thoughts and feelings onto another, non-human, creature. But I like the way it gently challenges the assumption we make, one which we have just as little basis for, that a short life must inevitably also be nasty and brutish. Even some human beings have been able to express the beauty of life, of God, in a life that is short. But perhaps we are in danger of thinking that the Mayfly's whole life is defined only by her final, adult, stage. In fact she spends most of her existence as an aquatic nymph. In this form she tunnels in the beds of ponds, lakes and slow-moving stretches of river. She is about one third as long again as her male counterpart and in favourable conditions can get to just over three centimetres. Local environment is everything to her. She may reach maturity in a year, or take three years, depending on her location (colder means longer). She emerges from her burrow in spring, moving instinctively towards shallow water. Over the last two weeks of May, perhaps as late as June (her name suggests that we have seen some climate fluctuation over the past few centuries) she begins the process of "eclosion" (leaving the water to "hatch"), between mid-morning and early afternoon.

Even with such a short adult lifespan, Mayflies still manage to be somebody's prey, most commonly Grayling and Trout, and it is on their way to the surface that most of her kind are taken. But if she successfully avoids these hunters she will shed her skin at the surface and undergo a brief (even by Mayfly standards) adolescent period of "subimago" or "dun" as she transitions into the adult, "spinner", stage. Drawn instinctively into the column of swarming males not far from the water's edge, the first to encounter her will fly up underneath, grasping her thorax with his legs and mate with her in the air. In the late afternoon he releases her and she returns to the water, skimming over its surface, touching it briefly and each time laying her eggs. Again the fish below try to seize their chance but she is quick and stops only for an instant. It is her they want and the eggs, or at least some of them, which drift to the bottom. Her task complete, her energy spent, she allows the surface of the water to catch her, falling and perhaps fluttering for a short time until the fish take her. Like her adulthood, her end is quick.

Populations and the number of different species on Britain's waterways have both declined since the 1970s, probably owing to pollution, especially agricultural runoff, against which they have little resistance,[89] so improving water quality will be good for Mayflies as well as other creatures, including ourselves. Unless you are a landowner your best course of action is to switch to buying organic produce. Although organic slurry can itself be a problem, farmers who work at being organic are usually aware of this kind of pitfall. One or two of the high-end supermarkets have done a lot to help smaller-scale, organic farms but it is worth talking to your local shopkeepers as well and to think about reducing your consumption of meat, which also massively affects your carbon footprint (Vegans have my blessing if they choose to look smug at this point). If you are not fearful of accidents with very young children and have the space, think about creating a pond in your garden. If you are very fortunate and have a stream running through your land, have a look and see if you can sensitively create the right conditions for this amazing and beautiful creature to move in. And if you cannot do any of the above, why not find out from your local Wildlife Trust or Angling Club when the best day is to see the Mayflies dance and just go to watch and wonder?

## From Luke 6:27-36 (NRSV)

*But I say to you that listen, Love your enemies, do good to those who hate you, bless those who curse you, pray for those who abuse you. If anyone strikes you on the cheek, offer the other also; and from anyone who takes away your coat do not withhold even your shirt. Give to everyone who begs from you; and if anyone takes away your goods, do not ask for them again. Do to others as you would have them do to you.*

*If you love those who love you, what credit is that to you? For even sinners love those who love them. If you do good to those who do good to you, what credit is that to you? For even sinners do the same. If you lend to those from whom you hope to receive, what credit is that to you? Even sinners lend to sinners, to receive as much again. But love your enemies, do good, and lend, expecting nothing in return. Your reward will be great, and you will be children of the Most High; for he is kind to the ungrateful and the wicked. Be merciful, just as your Father is merciful.*

## For Reflection and Prayer

Without any experience the Mayfly takes to the wing, instinctively timing her arrival in the swarm to perfection, negotiating wind and currents, avoiding skilled predators, using only the energy in her body (for she has no mouthparts, no way or time to eat). All this has been written into her nature by the Creator, all that is essential is already hers and her adult life is all focussed upon this one goal: to release the precious eggs and so continue the great dance of life. We too have all we need, the image of the Artist who is painting our lives, each of us unique but also part of a phenomenon that is humanity. It is this gift – and the knowledge of it – that enables us to follow the otherwise hard teaching above. For every human being, Christ has already accomplished what is essential. We simply have to receive it.

There is a strange paradox here: that we *learn* to live by the instinct that is naturally ours, restored to us through the work of the Spirit of God.

# Chapter 33

# Common Orb Weaver – entrusting the future to God

*the spider can be grasped in the hand,*
*yet it is found in kings' palaces*
– Proverbs 30:28

As you may have realised, the challenge in writing this book lay not in finding 40 native species but in working out who to include and who to leave out. Very early in the project I determined not to choose but to allow creatures to choose themselves. This one appeared unexpectedly in the base of a bird feeder I was about to fill and remained there for at least two weeks. Writing in October meant that I saw several, but I had not known the proper name for them, or the fact that the Orb Weavers are a large group comprising three and a half thousand species.

She is well known throughout western and central Europe, where she is native, and in North America where she has been introduced. She can be seen between May and November, although I find that summer is almost gone before she appears in numbers. Spinning her characteristic spoked-wheel web and often, though not always, sitting at its centre (her other tactic is to shelter in a hiding place at its edge, using a "communication thread" to pick up the telltale vibrations of prey), she is remarkably attuned. Simply blowing on the web or touching it with a stick will not lure her out of hiding. But try dropping a tiny bit of leaf onto it and watch. With surgical precision she will come and cut out the offending foreign body and let it drop to the ground. So she models sensitivity and discernment, moving when required and remaining still yet alert. This stillness protects her from predators (although I did watch one get larger day by day until, one morning, I found the web only with a large, suspiciously bird-sized hole punched right through the middle).

*Can papyrus grow where there is no marsh?*
*Can reeds flourish where there is no water?*
*While yet in flower and not cut down,*
*they wither before any other plant.*
*Such are the paths of all who forget God;*
*the hope of the godless shall perish.*
*Their confidence is gossamer,*
*a spider's house their trust*
*– Job 8:11-14*

In fact rebuilding her web is a normal chore for this relentless creature. Wind and rain, passing animals, erstwhile prey large enough to break free – all of these can put her in the position of having to start again, which she seems to do without fuss. It puts me in mind of some advice I was given about prayer: "If you find you have become distracted, do not waste time in regret, simply return to your prayer". A wise person once said we do not have to make our minds wander; they do that on their own. So, like the Orb Weaver, we return to the work of spinning our prayer before God in the hope of catching the Spirit's grace, our daily bread.

## From Luke 12:16-18, 20-21, 22, 24, 27-28, 32-34 (NRSV)

*Then he told them a parable: "The land of a rich man produced abundantly. And he thought to himself, 'What should I do, for I have no place to store my crops?' Then he said, 'I will do this: I will pull down my barns and build larger ones" ...But God said to him, 'You fool! This very night your life is being demanded of you. And the things you have prepared, whose will they be?' So it is with those who store up treasures for themselves but are not rich toward God."*

*..."Therefore I tell you, do not worry about your life, what you will eat, or about your body, what you will wear. For life is more than food, and the body more than clothing. Consider the ravens ... they have neither storehouse nor barn, and yet God feeds them ... Consider the lilies, how they grow: they neither toil nor spin; yet I tell you, even Solomon in all his glory was not clothed like one of these. But if God so clothes the grass of the field, which is alive today and tomorrow is thrown into the oven, how much more will he clothe you — you of little faith!*

*..."Do not be afraid, little flock, for it is your Father's good pleasure to give you the kingdom. Sell your possessions, and give alms. Make purses for yourselves that do not wear out, an unfailing treasure in heaven, where no thief comes near and no moth destroys. For where your treasure is, there your heart will be also."*

## For reflection and prayer

The web of the spider is an equivocal image. The prophet Isaiah (59:5) uses it as a way of describing how corrupt people weave a web of deceit. It is often used around Hallowe'en, although these are of course cobwebs, long abandoned by their creators and so perhaps appropriately they stand for death, the only truly static state. Webs and cobwebs generally indicate a place that has been left undisturbed. Perhaps one of the more famous examples is the web spun across a cave entrance on the Isle of Arran in which Robert the Bruce was hiding. Not only did this cause those who were hunting him to believe the place undisturbed, but the tenacity of the creature is said to have inspired him to continue at what was a low ebb in his life. So the spider is the subject of many projections, but what I would like to point to is the dynamic nature of her existence. The web she spins is integral to her life and survival and yet it is a temporary thing. Like the creatures Jesus speaks about she depends on what comes her way (she does actually toil *and* store, but you get the point). The bottom line here is that life is provisional. We cannot expect to reach a static place of total security. Whatever we build – as Job discovered – can be suddenly swept away. The wise person knows this but it does not stop her from building or creating. The knowledge that our work is temporary (even stone structures eventually crumble to dust) can leave us feeling hopeless. Only when we let go of the need to be eternal do we find that nothing is lost. The Common Orb Weaver lives to give birth and, having done so, she remains with the eggs until she dies. She literally gives her life away to protect them. In the same way, can we give ourselves fully to the creative work that is ours, and entrust the future to God?

# Chapter 34

# Meteorite – the deep silence of the Ancient of Days

Next year will be the five hundredth anniversary of her arrival on planet Earth, and yet this period – so many generations of humans – is a tiny fraction of her existence. She is not merely older than anything living on Earth, she is as old as Earth itself. She is an alien presence come among us from outer space and you can go and see her. You can even touch her.

The Nantan meteorite, so called because she was recovered from Nantan in China's Guangxi Province, weighs around 71 Kg (just over 155 lbs). She is composed mostly of iron and contains kamacite and taenite (alloys of iron and nickel). Her outer surface has been significantly changed by exposure to our atmosphere: on entry the friction caused by travelling through the air at very high speed melted her surface, giving her a more aerodynamic shape, a dark polished "fusion crust" and a large number of dimples (regmaglypts). In places the crust has eroded away and here the exposed iron has rusted (iron oxide).

I have chosen this creature to represent Rocks in general because the vast distances she has travelled at unimaginable speeds takes us into their realm, what might be referred to as "deep time". Formed before the ancestor of any living thing came into being on the earth, their age staggers the imagination. If they were to be given voice, what might they teach us? Would they speak to human beings? We are more ephemeral to them than the Mayfly is to us. Even the trees are like newborns in comparison. As with so many of the creatures in this series, most of us take their presence for granted on a daily basis, yet they have an enormous impact upon our daily life. We mine them for minerals, quarry them for blocks, crush them to make all kinds of things from pills to cement, smelt them for metals, tunnel into them for exploration, machine them for buildings, polish them for beauty. Broken into soil by plants, eroded by wind and wave and river, cracked apart by alternating heat and cold, they may be the most varied and the most mysterious creatures of all. And this mystery is not because of what we do not know but because of what we *do* know. They contain complex minerals and structures. Crack them open and we may find diamond, jade, amethyst, chrysotile, quartz... in fact there are over four thousand known minerals[90] and new ones are being added to the list every year. Any rock you encounter, from the ancient pillars of Stonehenge to the gravel on your neighbour's driveway, has witnessed the passage of thousands of generations of creatures, the rise and fall of whole civilisations, the emergence and extinction of species, ages of extreme cold and heat, periods and places in which life is impossible. And this individual, by forces beyond our knowledge, broken from who knows what planet in ancient time, spun into the tug of our Sun and would have become one with that boiling mass had our planet not drifted across her trajectory.

These were my thoughts as I sat resting my hand on the Nantan meteorite in Oxford's Museum of Natural History, a creature four and a half *billion* years old, unable to get beyond the fact that what lay beneath my palm – dark, almost matt black, with a metallic sheen, dimpled but not particularly rough and, as far as I could judge, incredibly dense – seems, more than anything else in the museum, to be rather dull.

I guess to many creatures I may seem rather dull too. Now in my mid-forties, even my own kind describe me as "middle-aged". It is amazing to think that the two of us – me and this meteorite may have met in the mid-point of both our existences, one less than a century, the other spanning ages of ages. She sits solidly upon her wooden plinth, suffering the touch of thousands of human beings; she seems perfectly still, perfectly silent.

## From Luke 19:29-30, 36-40 (NRSV)

*When he had come near Bethphage and Bethany, at the place called the Mount of Olives, he sent two of the disciples, saying, "Go into the village ahead of you, and as you enter it you will find tied there a colt that has never been ridden...."*

*As he rode along, people kept spreading their cloaks on the road.... the whole multitude of the disciples began to praise God joyfully with a loud voice for all the deeds of power that they had seen, saying,*

*"Blessed is the king*
*who comes in the name of the Lord!*
*Peace in heaven,*
*and glory in the highest heaven!"*

*Some of the Pharisees in the crowd said to him, "Teacher, order your disciples to stop." He answered, "I tell you, if these were silent, the stones would shout out."*

### For reflection and prayer

The irony of his days in Jerusalem must have weighed heavily on Jesus. For a long time he had known that it would be here that he would face his greatest trial, the fulfilment of his baptism which was, itself, a prophetic action of what was to come. Arriving at the high point in the year, the great celebration, bearing such knowledge must have felt so strange. He joined crowds from all over the known world, gathering to celebrate the rescue of God's people from Egypt. For most the festival also brought into sharp focus a huge political tension too: the hope that the God of the Exodus would bring about a new Exodus in their own day. The atmosphere would have been joyful, hopeful, intoxicating. In the midst of this he knew he would bring about God's rescue, and most of the people who were to witness it would not understand it until later. Some never would.

In William Horwood's *Duncton Wood* series of novels the moles worship and commune with a sacred stone and in so many ways our experience of God is like this. God seems immovable, eternal. We come with our questions and meet with long and deep silence. God does not seem moved by our sense of urgency, "a thousand years are like a day". Yes the rocks do indeed cry out, but their song is deep and slow and echoes from the earliest time. Even more than the trees, they set us in the same context as astronomy, whose vast distances remind us of our smallness, our temporariness. We have already seen that this is nothing to fear, but it is an awareness we need to learn to hold.

Rocks are among the oldest creatures in existence. Some contain the fossilised bodies of other creatures. Many have undergone incredible pressure or extreme heat, or been ground down by the pounding of waves only to be re-formed as sediment in the sea floor. So although what we see seems solid and eternal, they too are in a constant state of transformation, even this museum exhibit. She may spend decades, even centuries, on display and this would still barely scratch the surface of her existence. So what we learn is that everything – *everything* – changes. It is just that some creatures are taking their time.

It is particularly amusing therefore that, knowing all this, we still use phrases like "set in stone" or the even more ludicrous "concrete" to suggest permanence. The historically rather recent practice of erecting gravestones in churchyards itself shows that nothing is permanent. If you don't believe me take a stroll around your nearest graveyard (often wonderful places for wildlife, so worth a visit anyway) and look at the oldest examples. How does the realisation that nothing is static or permanent affect your self-understanding? How does it affect your relationship with the world of which you are a part? How does it affect your relationship with Jesus?

# Chapter 35

# Fox – awareness of self and environment

Some creatures are so iconic, and so well-documented, that it seems a bit more than cheeky to attempt a short chapter on them. Fox is one such, and yet how could I not? His absence would be an affront to a creature who deserves incredible respect and understanding. And, in the course of writing this book, on 4th October 2014 – the very day when the first gathering of our Forest Church took place – a Fox quite literally crossed my path.

My job starts in the early morning and by this time of the year it is night when I set off, cycling the 2 miles from home. One stretch of road is a long downhill swoop flanked by majestic Lime trees. It was on this gentle descent that a young Fox dashed out from a front garden on my left, passing inches from my advancing front wheel, and sped like an arrow into the hedge opposite. I have seen her before, but not often, usually at such a distance that it could have been a cat. This was the closest encounter with a Fox I have ever had.

Is it significant? Just the night before I had read Paul Cudby's chapter in a book entitled *Earthed*,[91] in which he describes another, even more exciting, close encounter. Paul goes on to quote the Guardian Columnist and author Graham Harvey:[92]

... owls, herons and crows are not rare in Britain, but I have witnessed them fly in ways that have been taken to indicate participation and benediction on Pagan celebrations ... the unusual physical proximity that sometimes occurs in encounters between particular birds and particular humans can be considered to be deliberate acts of communicative intimacy.

Ok, it wasn't a moment in which I would say I was in a state of prayer, although I do pray in the morning and am open to what I meet, and I was certainly not involved in a ritual at that moment, but it left me agape and wondering. In the same chapter, Paul talks about how two trees – whose folklore puts them in opposition – have begun to grow together among the roots of a Cedar that overshadows Ancient Arden Forest Church's regular gatherings: a sign of reconciliation. Some may say this is a coincidence, and perhaps it is, but if we are to recover our connection to nature we must pay heed to the non-rational[93] instincts we have, mindful that unexpected messengers do come to make us aware of something important. Perhaps the most stark example of this is in the book of Numbers, chapter 22, when a donkey sees an angel that his rider cannot. In the course of writing this book, I have taken time to look at shamanic and animist websites, and one theme that comes up time and again is what it may mean when a particular creature "crosses your path". Of course my inner sceptic asks whether this is not all just (over) interpretation, but then I have to ask why do humans have this capacity to notice and interpret certain events as signs in the first place? It is certainly an ability Jesus encourages us to explore and develop. So I choose not to ignore the presence of Fox on that birth-day of Cheltenham Forest Church, but I will keep it in mind and reflect upon it, open to what the Holy Spirit may be saying.

He knows his locality intimately. He checks it every night, making sure the scents and sounds are the same, alert to even slight changes. Moving our chicken house every few days meant that the foxes that ran through our garden on a nightly basis steered well clear and we never had any trouble. Like many hunters he is able to focus totally on a single point. Intelligent and creative, he is hard to track for very long and can seem to vanish. I once saw one from my car – a very large animal indeed – that stood in the middle of the road and looked straight at me, unflinching, forcing me to stop. Then he turned and I can only say *sauntered* through the hedge at the roadside. I got out to look and could find no opening in that hedge anywhere. It was, as far as I could see, utterly impenetrable. If the meeting in October was the closest, that was certainly the eeriest! The fact that he is a night-creature means that contemplating him also takes us into the shadows, the dream-world, of ourselves, as do some of the other creatures in these pages.

No doubt every fox identifies several hiding places, perhaps also developing some of them with a little digging or moving of foliage. These enable him to go to ground at a moment's notice and, if necessary, to lie low for a long time. He is a skilled predator and has, justifiably, earned a reputation for cunning. The flipside is, of course, that he is not entirely trusted, but I do find it strange that whenever I tell someone we keep chickens, they will invariably mention foxes. My instinct is that this is really a winter problem, when food sources are low and the young males in particular have not yet established themselves and are looking for their own territory.

It is always tempting to bring in the big guns to solve what we see as a problem. As *The Fox Project* [94] website points out, this only really provides a temporary solution, as destroying a terri-torial creature simply creates a vacuum for another to move in. It may even make matters worse, as a lot of the behaviours people dislike are related to establishing, rather than keeping, a territory. If you want to exclude foxes from your garden completely, there are artificial scent-marking products that will fool foxes into thinking someone else is there already. *The Fox Project* is not impressed with ultrasonic devices. Its main argument, based on research, is that fox populations are self-regulating. Unlike some other difficult species, you will not see an increase if they are left alone. Deter them humanely from your own patch and they will do the work of keeping other foxes away. They will also help to keep rodents in check. The intro-duction of wheelie bins has reduced their interference with our waste, which is good for them as well as us. But they are far more omnivorous than many people realise: beetles, Crane Flies, Earthworms, Blackberries, Apples and Pears are all part of a diet that also includes small mammals, birds and carrion. Any disease they carry may be partly our fault, as it is our food waste that is so problematic. It is no different from domestic dogs eating too much of our food. Something like sixty per cent of foxes are killed by cars, so driving a bit more slowly and not throwing edible rubbish – apple cores and the like – out of the car window will all help in a small way. And please refrain from putting out food for them, as this will artificially raise the population density (territories are smaller where food is more abundant). It is worth knowing that your dogs or cats (if you have them) are avoided by foxes, and there is no evidence that foxes attack either.

## From John 2:23-24; 6:2, 5-11, 14-15 (NRSV)

*When he was in Jerusalem during the Passover festival, many believed in his name because they saw the signs that he was doing. But Jesus on his part would not entrust himself to them, because he knew all people and needed no one to testify about anyone; for he himself knew what was in everyone.*

*... A large crowd kept following him, because they saw the signs that he was doing for the sick.... When he looked up and saw a large crowd coming toward him, Jesus said to Philip, "Where are we to buy bread for these people to eat?" He said this to test him, for he himself knew what he was going to do.... One of his disciples, Andrew, Simon Peter's brother, said to him, "There is a boy here who has five barley loaves and two fish. But what are they among so many people?" Jesus said, "Make the people sit down." Now there was a great deal of grass in the place; so they sat down, about five thousand in all. Then Jesus took the loaves, and when he had given thanks, he distributed them to those who were seated; so also the fish,*

*as much as they wanted.*

*When the people saw the sign that he had done, they began to say, "This is indeed the prophet who is to come into the world." When Jesus realized that they were about to come and take him by force to make him king, he withdrew again to the mountain by himself.*

## For reflection and prayer

Can we be as mindful of our environment as the Fox? Have you identified the safe places, the bolt holes, where you can pause if needs be? Do you know when "caution is the better part of valour", and it is right to slip away? With experience and prayerful reflection we too can map the territory, be it historical, physical or spiritual (and many situations call for an awareness of all three). The adult Fox does not make use of a Spiritual Director or Soul Friend as we can, but in infancy and youth the young shadow a parent and learn by observation. Such people are a vital resource, someone who can walk with you over familiar and new ground, who can help you better understand yourself and what may be needed at the present time. It helps if this person has some experience of counselling, although the two disciplines are not quite the same. In counselling we seek to help individuals (and more rarely couples or families) to function better in their situations. It may include setting goals, addressing the past (especially things that are unresolved), identifying patterns of behaviour and so on. In Spiritual Direction we are looking at a person's relationship with God, what God might be saying to that person at the present time. Many involved in this work (including me) dislike the word "director", which implies a certain authority or control, and prefer the term "accompaniment". In fact I would suggest that the word "spiritual" is also tricky, because there is an important earthiness about Jesus – let's not forget that he took flesh after all – a groundedness that is very much about what we do in the real world. We in the Christ

Tradition do not seek to escape, as some do, to some other, more spiritual, realm. That is not to say we are unspiritual, but the two exist together, not in conflict, and I would even say not really in tension.

## Chapter 36

# Adder – facing our depths

It is the bright day that brings forth the adder
And that craves wary walking.
– *Julius Caesar*, Act 2, Scene 1

I know of about three people's experiences with this creature that are almost exactly the same. One of them was my Dad's, one was mine and I heard about the third just last year. I was 25 and, uncertain about my future, had gone to stay for a week at Hilfield Friary, the mother house of the (Anglican) Society of St Francis, in Dorset. I told the brothers that I was not exactly on retreat but that I needed a break and some space. In fact I wanted not only to make room for prayer and my journal, but also to look closely at the community to decide if the "religious life", as it is called, was something I was called to (it wasn't). It was high summer and, following the Guest Brother's suggestion, on one particularly bright still day I walked from there to Cerne Abbas, a distance of about 5 miles. It was as I reached the crest of a small rise, near the edge of a field that I instinctively stopped dead in my tracks. There, directly in front of me, exactly where my foot was about to land was an Adder, basking in the sun. The strange thing about this experience was that I had not seen her, or was not aware that I had. Some other sense had warned me of her presence.

I forgot all about it until, some years later, Dad recounted just such an experience, in a different place but in almost all other details exactly the same. He did not know that this had happened to me, so when he told the story it was quite uncanny, as if my voice was coming from someone else. Since then I have heard a third person say almost the same thing: sensing rather than seeing the creature the moment before nearly treading on him or her. Is this a sense within us, or is it something the Adder is able to somehow transmit?

Snakes have not enjoyed a very good press in Christendom, owing to too literal a reading of what is clearly an allegorical tale in the opening chapters of the book of Genesis. I want to be clear about this: it seems obvious to me that the story of Eve and the Fruit of the Tree of Knowledge (it was <u>not</u> an apple, folks!) is an allegory, a creation myth rich in archetypes, with אָדָם (Adam) meaning "Earth-creature", חַוָּה (Eve – actually Chava, Chaya or Chawwa, where the "ch" is pronounced gutturally) meaning "Living". Together they become "Living Earth Creature", echoing the note sounded in Genesis 2:7; "*then the Lord God formed man from the dust of the ground and breathed into his nostrils the breath of life; and the man became a living being*" (NRSV). The garden stands for Creation and the relationship we have with God. After all, if the snake is Satan and it all happened literally, why bother calling him "the snake"? In any event it was not an Adder, and we have some catching up to do.

She is Britain's only venomous snake and one of only three snakes that are native. The others are Grass Snakes and Smooth Snakes. Her poison is generally reserved for prey (voles, shrews, other reptiles, frogs, newts, snails and chicks that have either fallen or been pushed from nests or those who belong to ground-nesting species such as Meadow Pipit and Skylark, eggs of course and insects) although it can be used as a defence. But she would always choose retreat rather than a fight, as is true of most animals. The alternative is costly and involves too much risk (only humans seem foolish enough to let confrontations escalate, but we do love to project this violence and stupidity onto others). Feeding is a laborious process of swallowing the prey whole after it has expired and powerful digestive juices dissolve every-thing, even the bones, and presumably neutralize the poison.

Her underground hibernation site, which she uses every year, will almost certainly be the place of her birth. When she was young she found it by following the scent trail of other Adders. So perhaps she teaches us something about rootedness that we have lost. Her mother may have travelled up to one kilometre from her own hibernation site after mating. Unlike most British animals birth happens at the end of the summer rather than in springtime, and she hatched out of the egg whilst still inside her mother's body. Early spring is the best time to go looking for her at woodland edges, on moorland, grassland or heaths and if you are very fortunate you may see an "Adder dance", once thought to be a precursor to mating but actually a struggle for dominance between two males. She will be at least five years old if she is ready to mate, and can live to fifteen. If she becomes a mother, giving birth to up to ten young at a time, she will not mate again for another two years. On sunny days, as I found out first-hand, she likes to soak up the heat, relying on her markings – the characteristic zigzag down her back – that either breaks up his outline or serves as a warning to stay away. Otherwise she is secretive and hides in the burrows and holes left by other animals. She has to watch out for Badger, Fox and Owls, all of whom will kill her if they can. Perhaps this is the reason why she is often associated with secret knowledge and, by extension, magic.

Hibernation, coupled with the habit of shedding her skin shortly thereafter, traditionally associates the Adder with renewal and rebirth and, as we see with other creatures, there is a sense of moving between worlds – in this case between the land of shadows and the world of light.

If you do see one please do not approach as s/he will perceive you as a threat and move away. Too much of this can threaten the individual's survival,[95] apparently, although I am not sure exactly why. Because the females travel to give birth in new sites it is important not to let their habitats become separated by such things as change of use, development or roads. That means it is not enough to preserve the wood the Adders are found in but also its surroundings. This kind of thinking has been sadly lacking in the UK where, as I have said elsewhere, we seem to think nature belongs only in special reserves rather than recognising nature is a living phenomenon we are part of. If you see Adders please report them to your local Wildlife Trust,[96] who will be able to use this knowledge as part of their land management and lobbying councils and government for better sensitivity in land use.

### From John 3:1-3, 14-15 (NRSV)

*Now there was a Pharisee named Nicodemus, a leader of the Jews. He came to Jesus by night and said to him, "Rabbi, we know that you are a teacher who has come from God; for no one can do these signs that you do apart from the presence of God." Jesus answered him, "Very truly, I tell you, no one can see the kingdom of God without being born from above" ... "And just as Moses lifted up the serpent in the wilderness, so must the Son of Man be lifted up, that whoever believes in him may have eternal life."*

### For reflection and prayer

I remain open about his ability to convey some kind of warning. This may be something he can do, or it may be that humans have a strong programming to recognise snakes at the periphery of our vision, or by some other sense we are not fully aware of. I do believe that there are instincts and senses that, in our urbanized and fragmented culture, lie dormant, and that a combination of awareness exercises and prayer is needed in order to reawaken ourselves to a greater connection with our true selves. This 'self' lies beyond the individual identity and everyday consciousness.

I am the pattern of fear, and its overcoming
– from MED Theatre's, *Martha and the Snake*[97]

The Adder occupies a significant place in our folklore (her name has changed from the Old English Naeddre, and in Welsh she is called Nathair) and it is suggested that she has an ancient enmity with the Ash tree, although I cannot find the basis of that tale.

Because snakes are one of a number of more common phobias, the snake may represent the things we would rather turn away from, such as uncertainty or a particular fear. Like any fear, the reality is far less threatening that what we imagine. The story of the snake (not an Adder but certainly venomous) lifted up in the desert is told in the book of Numbers (21:4-9) is one of the strangest signs in the Bible, almost the opposite of what you would expect. The refugee people speak (with forked tongues?) against their leaders and, in consequence, God sends snakes among them. Many die from the bites until Moses, under God's instruction, makes a snake of bronze which people only have to look at to be cured. This is the story Jesus refers to. Is he really describing himself as a kind of snake that brings healing to all who look upon him? At his crucifixion the author of John's Gospel cites a verse from the prophet Zechariah: "They will look on the one whom they have pierced". Looking upon Christ on the cross confronts us with everything we wish to deny about ourselves. This denial runs so deeply that to face it "could be a huge threat to [our] self-concept".[98] So Jesus enables us to do something we cannot do, to recover our sensitivity, facets of our being that we have lost touch with over generations, and to face the depths that are within us. As we do so he also enables us to find forgiveness, whether we are able to fully grasp this reality or not.

# Chapter 37

# Chicken of the Woods – looking at the heart

There are many species of bracket fungi and, unsurprisingly, they have some things in common. Some of them are given rather unattractive names like "Ash heart rot", "Beech heart rot", "Top Rot", "Butt Rot" ...you get the idea. It is enough to make anyone feel a bit queasy. But who can resist a smile when they first encounter this flamboyant creature, the Sulphur Polypore, also known as "Chicken of the Woods"?

As with mushrooms, what you are seeing is the fruiting body of the fungus. Some brackets can grow to a couple of feet wide, but this one usually tops out at just over half that. They always look rather delicate but take hold of one, especially if it is older, and you will find it feels pretty much like an old boot and is almost as tough. They are an indication that a fungus has become pretty well established in a tree, and each bracket will release millions of spores which, carried by the wind, establish new fungal colonies in any wounded trees they encounter. However, while some trees seem more susceptible to fungal infection, others have the ability to fight back or at least to limit the internal spread. Human interventions, no matter how well-meaning, often do more harm than good.[99] In fact one of the big questions we have to ask in any natural setting is whether we are meant to "intervene" at all. This is most often apparent during wildlife documentaries, where it is obvious that a little assistance by the camera crew can mean the difference between life and death. As a creature with a moral sense, this is a dilemma we have to live with, but it is easy for us to be misguided, either because we "anthropomorphise" the situation (define everything in human terms) or because we fail to grasp the whole picture. It is easier to divide the world into the good, the bad and the ugly, but real life isn't like that.

In any event the Sulphur Polypore is certainly not ugly. His bracket has the lovely, irregular shape of a discarded duvet, sunny yellow on the underside with a more orangey hue on top. Oh, and, as long as the individual is not growing on Yew (which infuse him with poison) you can eat it.[100] He is found in and on Oak, Sweet Chestnut, Poplar, Willow, Yew and Cherry Trees, often in a tiered stack, like a pile of Canadian pancakes. It is unlikely that you will see him in the spring, so make a note in your diary to go walking in late summer/early autumn (easily the best time to go walking in any case).

We could see the interaction between bracket fungi and trees as somewhat like the predator/prey relationship. He encourages the vitality of the forest by picking off the weaker individuals. This also helps militate against monocultures (where one species excludes all others), which is never a healthy arrangement (even though it is the one favoured by almost all arable farmers). It is interesting to see that bracket fungi play something of a "long game", attacking the heartwood rather than the living tissue. This means that a tree may live with the "condition" for years, even decades, before the progressive disappearance of her core renders her unstable. Even then a fallen tree may throw new shoots upwards, and this means she has every chance of reproducing and supporting other life or, to use the Biblical term, "bearing fruit". The fungus himself changes role through this process, beginning as a parasite (living off another living creature) and then becoming a saprophyte (living off a dead creature). During the age of sail, Chicken of the Woods would sometimes appear on the bulkheads of British warships, usually a sign that the wood was so far rotted that it needed urgent replacement.

Does he taste like chicken? Some say so. He has also been described variously as "lemony", "meaty", "mushroomy" (no surprises there), "like crab", and "like lobster". There are two ways to find out: one is to eat some, the other is to feed it to someone you trust (and who presumably trusts you) and let them tell you.

We badly need more extensive woodland in this country, chiefly because we now know that forests, especially in the temperate zones, play a vital role in regulating the climate. We also need them to restore some balance to our lives, which have become so barren. Simply increasing the amount of natural woodlands will provide plenty of openings for this opportunist, who occurs throughout the UK and is not endangered. I would also suggest that our parks and open spaces are far too sterile. We need more wildness and because some humans – a tiny but far too influential minority – can make these places seem unsafe, we need a new courageousness too, to get out and use public spaces and ensure that their atmosphere is not tainted by a few maladjusted individuals. In any case, antisocial behaviour arises from a sense of disconnection. The more wilderness we can reintroduce, the better connected people will be. I am not saying the problems will solve themselves, but it is far better to invite people to a better future than to threaten them with punishments.

It may seem odd to suggest this, but I also think a significant thing we can do for Chicken of the Woods is to eat some, which is an exercise in trust (although you will be relieved to hear that nothing else looks like him so it really is hard to get wrong) and increases our connection with the food we eat – few things are as thoroughly disconnected as we are with the sources of our food – and dispels the silly but pervasive idea that "nature" is dirty and dangerous and needs to be thoroughly processed before we allow it to come near.

### From John 17:1-3, 6, 8, 20-23, 26 (NRSV)

*Jesus ... looked up to heaven and said, "Father, the hour has come;*

*glorify your Son so that the Son may glorify you, since you have given him authority over all people, to give eternal life to all whom you have given him. And this is eternal life, that they may know you, the only true God, and Jesus Christ whom you have sent....*

*"I have made your name known to those whom you gave me from the world ... for the words that you gave to me I have given to them, and they have received them and know in truth that I came from you; and they have believed that you sent me..."*

*"I ask not only on behalf of these, but also on behalf of those who will believe in me through their word, that they may all be one. As you, Father, are in me and I am in you, may they also be in us, so that the world may believe that you have sent me. The glory that you have given me I have given them, so that they may be one, as we are one, I in them and you in me, that they may become completely one, so that the world may know that you have sent me and have loved them even as you have loved me..."*

*"I made your name known to them, and I will make it known, so that the love with which you have loved me may be in them, and I in them."*

## For reflection and prayer

There are a number of parables in which Jesus suggests we cannot "root out" what is bad without losing what is good as well (see for example Matthew 13:24-30). What we see in the Sulphur Polypore and his host is a relationship that is established for good or ill. They are so interconnected that it would be impossible to separate them. While it is tempting to think of this as inherently bad – after all, who likes a parasite? – Jesus also shows us that our relationship with God is like this. There is a sense in which God "infects" us. God gets into our core, often through our imperfections and woundedness, and gets to work on the hardness within.

By the time it starts to show outwardly we have already become fused, one with God. You cannot really say where the human ends and God begins, it is all one. Or we can look at it another way, that the wounds of Christ allow us to get in, to graft ourselves onto the Kingdom and inhabit it, drawing life, bearing fruit and spreading the spores abroad of what we have become. Of course there are some who would say I am talking rot, but then there will always be those who look only at the surface. Do not let them trouble you. God looks at the heart.

## Chapter 38

# Oak – the gift of true community

One of the great icons of the British landscape, the Oak casts a giant shadow. Whether standing alone or in ancient woodland, there is an undeniable majesty about this creature who provides food, shelter and habitat for hundreds of other species. A German visitor to one of our Forest Church gatherings recently commented on how impressive the Oak trees were in Gloucestershire compared to those she sees at home, and yet here Oak rarely reaches her full potential. To see exactly how impressively they can grow you need to visit the Białowieża Forest World Heritage site,[101] where deep woodland has been allowed to establish unchecked for centuries. At the time of writing it remains an ambition of mine to visit this incredible place, whose forests show something of the way Britain used to be, when it was said a Squirrel could travel from the Severn to the Wash without touching the ground. Here massive Oaks can be seen, among the other species that make this region so impressive: creatures such as Wolf, Lynx and Bear that have long been absent from these islands, and Eagles, Owls, and Beavers, who remain rarities.

As a sapling her growth was rapid and vigorous. Now over a hundred years old, it has slowed considerably. But she still has the best part of life ahead of her. The Woodland Trust uses a wonderful phrase, "leaf burst", for the emergence of her foliage in the middle of May. The very opposite of Kingfisher[102] or Mayfly, Oak plays a long game, not producing acorns until around 40 years old and being at her most productive now, between 80 and 120. Perhaps there is a reminder here for us that it is not only in the sixth and seventh stages of life[103] that we can be fruitful. Once she starts to produce them, Oak showers an abundance of seeds upon the earth, an outpouring of food for Mice, Squirrels, Badgers, Deer of all kinds, Jays, Boar.... Indeed she supports more species than any other tree native to Britain: literally hundreds of different kinds of insects, and therefore many kinds of birds and bats and other mammals, many of whom will also be found nesting in the holes they either create or find in her trunk or dig between her roots. Where leaf fall is captured in a junction of branches mini-forests can form, tens of feet in the air. The humus beneath her is home to all manner of beetles and fungi and, like most trees, she also plays host to parasites such as the Mistletoe (the subject of another chapter) and the occasional colony of Bees (although her nectar is one of the few that they cannot touch).[104]

This symbiosis with so many other creatures means that Oak is one of a number of species that embodies the interconnectedness of the natural world. We can do far worse than rest in her shade, gather her leaves for wine-making or leaf mould, feed her acorns to pigs or grind some into flour for cooking, collect her fallen branches for firewood and carving, hang a rope swing or climb into her sturdy boughs to enjoy the view. In life her open structure allows light to filter through to the forest floor, allowing every layer of vegetation to be present. Even when she crashes to earth she gives life, creating a clearing that is the opportunity for all kinds of creatures to move in. Some of these will inhabit her decaying trunk; others will burrow underneath especially as winter approaches, while some (see Rosebay Willowherb) will grab the chance afforded by the light before being shaded out by her successors.

Although she rarely appears in heraldry, the Oak has long stood as a symbol of what is best, and most enduring, about Britain, and perhaps England in particular. Her hard, long-lasting timber has been fashioned into many a door, provided the supports and floor for many a large house and been the table around which many a family has gathered. A king fleeing into exile hid in one of her ancestors and later enshrined religious tolerance in law (although this may have had more to do with the fact that he was also sheltered by Roman Catholics). At that time it was normal for couples to wed under Oak trees. The tradition was to make vows to one another and *then* go to the church, meeting the priest under the lych gate – probably also constructed of Oak – to have the marriage formally recognised. The Book of Common Prayer service is actually called "The Solemnization of Matrimony". At Christmas the Yule Log would be a bough of Oak, kept burning throughout the season. Any that remained after the twelfth night would be kept until the following year to be used to start the next Yule fire.[105] Today we no longer use her tannin for leather-making but we continue to mature brandy and wine in oak barrels for the distinctive depth of flavour these impart.

In 2006 the Oak Processionary Moth began to appear in the UK,[106] yet another example of the devastation an invasive species can bring. They damage the leaves and make Oak more vulnerable to disease such as Acute Oak Decline (AOD) and Chronic Oak Decline (COD). They are actually quite unpleasant for humans too. Acute Oak Decline is an older problem, and has been around for about thirty years. It is characterised by dark weeping patches on the main stem. Openings in the bark, exposing the core wood underneath, are another obvious sign, often with clear damage to the latter. Research is ongoing but it is believed a particular species of beetle is a significant factor. Chronic Oak Decline has been in evidence for about a century and seems to be caused by fungal infection. Whilst AOD kills a tree in about four to five years, COD can take decades. While on a visit to the New Forest a few years ago, we came across efforts to tackle something called Sudden Oak Death, caused by a species thought to be associated with Rhododendrons (yes, another foreign plant introduced for decorative purposes). The best thing to do when confronted with any sick tree is to inform your local council.

So having said we can enjoy the oak as a kind of natural climbing frame, it is important not to do damage to her bark or to break bits off, as these create openings for disease to attack. Otherwise she is fairly robust and, as we have seen, common enough not to cause too much concern at the present time. Take time to stand in awe of this creature, who was probably here before you and will be here after you. Think about the many changes in your life and how this individual has stood here throughout all of them, a sign of the deep peace and faithfulness of God, who is with you in all things, on one hand untroubled by the changes all around, but also fully present come what may.

## From 1 Corinthians 12:12-15, 17, 21, 26 (NRSV)

*Just as the body is one and has many members ... so it is with Christ. For in the one Spirit we were all baptized into one body – Jews or Greeks, slaves or free – and we were all made to drink of one Spirit.*

*Indeed, the body does not consist of one member but of many. If the foot would say, "Because I am not a hand, I do not belong to the body," that would not make it any less a part of the body ... If the whole body were an eye, where would the hearing be? If the whole body were hearing, where would the sense of smell be? ... The eye cannot say to the hand, "I have no need of you," nor again the head to the feet, "I have no need of you." ... If one member suffers, all suffer together with it; if one member is honored, all rejoice together with it.*

### For reflection and prayer

Like all broadleaf deciduous trees, the Oak embodies death and resurrection through the seasons and this cycle also means a generous shower of nutrient into the soil all around. So generosity and symbiosis, true community, is the gift of this tree to us. She is a living reminder that we are called to give what we receive, and to let our lives be a constant flow to others. Note that I say "receive and give" here, which is quite different from the traditional phrase "give and take"; for we too are called to give our bodies back to the earth and allow other generations to rise. We so often think of this as sad, but it is not. The people of God at various points in the Bible, which itself covers an impressive span of history, use the phrase "the way of all flesh" to describe ageing and death. How often do we hear "life is too short" and worry about not getting everything done in time? This mindset makes us anxious and unproductive, filling our lives with busyness in the fear that we will die before we have achieved our goals. The Oak reminds us that, for most of us living in Britain today, life is long – a third of those born in 2013 are expected to live to be a century old[107] – and we are called to be generous with it. She also stands as a symbol of the unity and community of creation – which has gained a new emphasis in recent times through the work of James Lovelock, whose "Gaia Hypothesis" suggests that the world itself may be thought of as one body. Truly it may be said that "our life is with our neighbour".[108] The Oak underlines the point made elsewhere in this book – that there is no room for hatred of others (which has to do with a fundamental rejection of ourselves) as we follow Christ. Living generously, then, with thanksgiving and an awareness of the way this venerable creature looks kindly upon our youth, leads us to recover a joyfulness and lightness of living that we badly need.

# Chapter 39

# Common Hermit Crab – embracing change

Ogmore-by-Sea may be my idea of a perfect beach. The sand is of a texture that really holds together when digging sandcastles, there are rocks whose position at the meeting point of sea and land have led to fascinating wave and rainwater erosion, the beach itself grades gently into the tidal water, and there are rockpools.

Common Hermit Crabs are common all along the British coast, one of sixty-two crab species native to our shores.[109] There are fifteen species native to British coastal waters, eight of which are relatively easy to find (the rest are in deeper water). His species is both the largest and the most populous we have.

He is the surprise inhabitant of other creatures' shells, so just when you think you have made one discovery you find you have made another, just as delightful. For just as some land creatures take up residence in the abandoned burrows of others, this doughty neighbour takes full advantage of the litter of shells that his fellow coastal residents leave behind. He lives in the zone defined by the tides and as far out as 140m depth of water, and his size seems to be related to how deep he can go (smaller individuals are found in shallower water). His body is made up of two main sections: a "cephalothorax" (head and torso in one) and a spiral abdomen. Generally reddish or brown in colour, one pair of legs has become adapted to hold the shell in place until his natural growth makes it necessary to move to a larger one. This is, of course, an incredibly vulnerable process for him, and there are plenty of predators willing to take advantage of his exposure, so he moves as quickly as he can to insert his soft abdomen into the new shell. It is important that it is just the right size: too small and he will be restricted, too large and he will not be adequately protected. No doubt many of his kind die because of this lack. Good shells are highly significant and this has a big influence on Hermit Crab culture. He is a creature of quick decisions and timely action, changing to a new shell immediately if he believes it is better than the one he has.

He is a predator and an opportunist, sporting two large claws – one slightly larger than the other – used for hunting, gathering food and as weapons. He has compound eyes and four antennae. He is a real benefit to his ecosystem, aiding in the breakdown of large, dead organisms and playing his part in what are termed "nutrient cycles". His diet comprises tiny molluscs, algae, plankton and worms, and the leftovers of others' meals. In times of scarcity he will attack and eat his own kind. Among those queuing up to eat him are various birds including Seagulls, various fish, starfish, octopi and other crabs. There are also at least twenty-three different parasites that threaten him. It is a tough environment.

As a mature adult he is in the sixth stage of a life that has an expectancy of around four years. The other five were got through in just two months. When he finds a mate he will take hold of her using the smaller of his two claws and will hold on for hours or even days until she is ready. It is not clear whether her signal is chemical or physical, but the two then face one another, tapping each others' claws and mouthparts. Leaving their shells they copulate for a few minutes but then remain together for up to ten minutes before returning. There is no specific mating season. After copulation the female will produce two or three hundred black eggs, which she carries until they begin to hatch about six weeks later.

Elsewhere I have considered the problem of the word "common" in the names of creatures. Here we need to be aware of the potential confusion caused by the word "Hermit". In fact these crabs are intensely social. Active mostly at nighttime, he will gather with others and assess his relative dominance (the community always has a dominant male) first by looking, then by displays (raising his body and lifting his claws. The smaller of the two will lower his body, but if they are fairly evenly matched a fight is inevitable. This takes the form of a wrestling match in which the winner is the one who can get on top of the other's shell and deliver as many hard knocks with his claws as it takes for his opponent to submit.

I do not like the over-extensive use of the word "competition" beloved of so many who speak about other species, but there does appear to be a demand for good shells. Our friend will make a play, and fight, for a shell belonging to another if it appears to be desirable. He is able to remember shells he has seen before. Oddly, he seems to prefer shells with "epibionts" (creatures, such as anemones, who live on the shell) to those that appear clean. This may be because they also defend themselves against predators and so provide a second level of defence for him, or because they create better camouflage, or some other reason we do not know.

What can we do for Hermit Crab? As is so often the case, our first discipline is what we should *not* do. Please do not purchase one as a pet. As a rule Hermit Crabs do not breed successfully in captivity, so any you see on sale have been removed from the wild. Because they are social, owning one isolates a creature that needs the company of her or his fellows, and I doubt many of us have the capacity to accommodate a proper community of them. It is hard to create the conditions in which they thrive (especially the deep sand in which they moult), tap water contains elements that are toxic to them, traders often paint their shells for novelty value and this can also poison them. The story that their growth depends on the size of the tank you provide is a pernicious lie (and, frankly, absurd to anyone who thinks about it for even a moment). The pretty shells you so often see on sale in seaside shops will have been gathered (possibly trawled) from the sea bed, most likely near the coast which is rich in biodiversity, so buying these supports an industry that damages delicate ecosystems and robs Hermit Crabs of a vital resource. The other thing we should avoid is releasing pet Hermit Crabs back into the wild, as they may have picked up diseases that will spread to the wild population.

Hermit Crabs have not yet been assessed for conservation status, but they are not believed to be under threat at the present time. However, the pollution of coastal waters and insensitive activities and development are bound to have an effect on numbers and the well-being of individuals. The Marine Conservation Society[110] provides helpful guidelines to anyone who is planning to do a "Seashore Safari". So please do go looking in rockpools and the shallows, delight in the life you find there, and support any work that seeks to protect these dynamic habitats from the unnecessary damage caused by our kind.

## From 1 Peter 2:5-10 (NRSV)

*Like living stones, let yourselves be built[a] into a spiritual house, to be a holy priesthood, to offer spiritual sacrifices acceptable to God through Jesus Christ. For it stands in scripture:*
    *"See, I am laying in Zion a stone, a cornerstone chosen and precious;*
    *and whoever believes in him will not be put to shame."*
*To you then who believe, he is precious; but for those who do not believe, "The stone that the builders rejected has become the very head of the corner," and "A stone that makes them stumble, and a rock that makes them fall." They stumble because they disobey the word, as they were destined to do. But you are a chosen race, a royal priesthood, a holy nation, God's own people, in order that you may proclaim the mighty acts of him who called you out of darkness into his marvellous light. Once you were not a people, but now you are God's people; once you had not received mercy, but now you have received mercy.*

## For reflection and prayer

There is so much we can receive from encountering this fellow creature, but I am choosing on this occasion to think about defences. I was once advised that I needed very good defences for a particular role I had in an organisation. In fact that situation came to a very unsatisfactory conclusion. For me, the process of letting go of certain defences had been a valuable one, over many years, and I had come to trust ever more deeply in God. I had realised, some years earlier, that there is a relationship between trust and peace, although I still cannot tell you which comes first. This, I believe, is the gift of the Holy Spirit. So when my role required me to become cunning and defended again, I chose to continue on the path Christ had led me on. It was one of the hardest things I have ever had to do, but I do not regret it for a moment.

In our lives we naturally develop defences to cope with the things that come our way. Some of these are genuine threats, others perhaps more illusory though no less powerful. When our circumstances change we often carry our old defences into the new situation. If we are not careful we can even end up creating the same situations again and again, as part of those defences is the expectation that we will come under attack from the same quarter. To use an architectural analogy, the castles of Britain are impressive fortresses, perfect for controlling an occupied country or defending against raids. But they were always uncomfortable homes, and when more peaceful times came it made sense to adapt them, widening and glazing arrow slits to let the light in, draining stagnant moats to create gardens, turning armouries into bigger kitchens and partitioning large rooms to create bedrooms (it is an interesting fact that castles had almost no sleeping accommodation for their large number of inhabitants, most of whom slept in the main hall or in corridors). I am aware that speaking about buildings can play into a rather unhelpful tendency among Christians, and others who live in these countries with their shared Christian heritage, namely the idea of church buildings as "God's house". In fact Scripture does not have this fixed view. The house spoken about above is a work in progress, not something that has been finished, and it is an analogy for a holy *people*, not some kind of new temple that we go to in order to meet God. The Hermit Crab reminds us of this: we carry our spiritual home with us and are invited by Jesus to continue to grow, pilgrims on a journey, not to stagnate believing we have somehow "arrived", and not to believe that the purpose of life is to get to some fixed point where we no longer have to change.

# Chapter 40

# Eel – knowing our true home

Not all fish can manage both fresh and salt water, although some (Perch for example) may be found where the two meet. What sets the European Eel apart is that he may spend as long as twenty years in the fresh water environment here, despite the fact that his life began and ends at sea. What is more the "sea" in which he emerges and, at the end of his life, spawns and dies, itself migrates, having no land boundary. This is the Sargasso Sea, named for the Sargassum[111] plant that forms a vast floating mass (it occupies almost two thirds of the North Atlantic) in which all kinds of creatures make a temporary or permanent home. Its continual journey is bounded and driven by oceanic currents. A huge population inhabits the Sargasso Sea and other species, including Tuna and Humpback Whale, regularly migrate through it. The Eel is therefore a resident alien. His life is here, but he has written into the core of his being the deep knowledge of this "other country", and somehow he knows when it is time to return. The first three years of his life has been spent drifting in the ocean, one of thousands, first as a leaf-shaped baby, then, on arrival at the European continental shelf a tiny "glass eel", no more than a few centimetres long. By some urge not yet known to us, he turns towards this land. He enters our waterways. Still a mere seven centimetres in length, the young "elver" pushes upstream, feeding on invertebrates and then smaller fish. Over the years his body darkens and lengthens. Growing slowly, his mature form will be from sixty to eighty centimetres.

The discovery that we ourselves inhabit a migratory, pilgrim world is said to have changed forever our perception of ourselves. The sight of planet Earth from our only Moon – something never seen before – can evoke all kinds of feelings. We perhaps become aware of her comparative smallness in the vastness of space, of the fact that she is finite, that we are a community who must learn to live together. This sense of the world's apparent fragility may be pure projection. If James Lovelock is correct the world is, in fact, extremely resilient, with many of the characteristics of a single organism, including an apparent ability to heal, a drive towards balance. This is not really surprising. Life has existed here for eons. Even in the relatively short time humans have been around we have seen whole civilisations rise and fall, even those that have lasted for centuries. It makes eminent sense that life must either perpetuate itself or be sustained by something or someone. For your entire life you have been travelling through space at an astonishing speed. Every year of life has been a circuit of the Sun. Whether we are aware of it or not, we are all of us pilgrims, and we all have within us a deep awareness of where we have come from and a longing, when the course of our natural life is complete, to return.

In other traditions the Eel, who journeys in the deep, stands for spiritual awareness and sensitivity to life's "currents". His long body naturally points, arrow-like, and this is another aspect of pilgrimage: every journey has an end, a goal, in sight, and we turn our faces towards it, but pilgrimage also recognises the presence of Christ now. The journey itself is of value. Robert MacFarlane, in his book *The Wild Places*,[112] explores this helpfully as he looks at different maps. "The map is not the territory", so what is mapped often says more about the cartographer than the ground. It is what we choose to include, and what we leave out, that reflects our own priorities. An alien looking at a road atlas, for example, might be forgiven for thinking that there are no woods or hills, rivers or lakes, in the whole of Britain. But she would be more likely to conclude that these things do not matter to us, even that we want to block them out as we speed on our focussed way. The Eel does not make this mistake. Dwelling for so many years in this country, he is not just about getting back to the Sargasso Sea. For pretty much every animal seems to be able to completely inhabit the present moment, something we have to learn – or perhaps re-learn – as we grow through our adult lives. In terms of positive action, perhaps the most important thing we can do will not just help the Eel, because it is reckoned that climate change is bringing about changes in ocean currents and that may be preventing Eels migrating to Britain. Along with loss of suitable habitat, alterations to rivers that inhibit migration, pollution and over-fishing, it has caused a massive drop in the numbers coming here, up to 95 per cent in some rivers.[113] The International Union for Conservation of Nature (IUCN) lists the European Eel as critically endangered. We need to recognise that our fate is intricately bound up with the fate of others. Climate change is a problem that requires a huge concerted effort of all peoples, a unity in the human family that has rarely, if ever, been achieved before (the last time was when a global ban on Chlorofluorocarbons, a family of chemical compounds used widely in refrigerators and aerosol sprays' which caused massive environmental damage, was introduced in 1987). We can all act at a personal level, making changes to our lifestyle, and we also have a great opportunity as members of a democracy. The Eel may not be the prettiest creature in human terms, but he is part of our community, one of us, and it is this sense of community and belonging that will be vital for us and for generations to come.

## From Ephesians 2:11-13; 3:14-19 (NRSV)

*So then, remember that at one time you Gentiles by birth, called "the uncircumcision" by those who are called "the circumcision" – a physical circumcision made in the flesh by human hands – remember that you were at that time without Christ, being aliens from the commonwealth of Israel, and strangers to the covenants of promise, having no hope and without God in the world. But now in Christ Jesus you who once were far off have been brought near by the blood of Christ....*

*... For this reason I bow my knees before the Father, from whom every family in heaven and on earth takes its name. I pray that, according to the riches of his glory, he may grant that you may be strengthened in your inner being with power through his Spirit, and that Christ may dwell in your hearts through faith, as you are being rooted and grounded in love. I pray that you may have the power to comprehend, with all the saints, what is the breadth and length and height and depth, and to know the love of Christ that surpasses knowledge, so that you may be filled with all the fullness of God.*

## For reflection and prayer

The Christ Community in Ephesus knew what it was to belong to another country. A well-established Roman outpost, they displayed many of the characteristics we see among expats even today. Paul wrote to show them that the true home from which they came – the true kingdom of which they were both an outpost and a signpost – was not a human empire but something far deeper and enduring, something that was with them and within them and also something towards which they were making a journey.

In the life of Jesus it appears that he wandered around the north of what we now call Israel (then the Roman province of Judea). He appeared in all kinds of places and even at one point slipped off to the very far north (today's Lebanon). But there came a point when he knew the time was right and from then on he headed for Jerusalem where the story of his life reached its climax.

In the same way we know that our time will come – and we hope it is after a long and fulfilling life – to make our own "homeward journey". But it is also true for us that sometimes a call comes that causes us to turn from the place we have been in and make a new start. Getting this right is one of the great challenges in life and faith. I have always enjoyed change, and so have probably moved too often. Many people have the opposite inclination and perhaps are too slow to move. It may be that there is no perfect way, and God knows this. We do not have the same instincts as the Eel. We are blessed (?) with a reasoning mind that has to work in concert with our instinct, but developing a prayerful, listening inner disposition is vital if we are to detect the currents of God's Spirit. Our prayer makes us ever more deeply aware of how completely loved we are, and it is this that moves us at the right time. So take some time, as indeed you have been doing, and know God.

# Conclusions

The journey of knowing continues, of course. These meditations are merely a series of steps on a much larger Way. I said at the start that I wanted to get scientific knowledge and study into dialogue with spiritual awareness and respect. I wonder what your experience of that process has been.

I also spoke about story, how for far too long our story has not only put us at the centre, it has actively excluded many (most?) of the essential characters. It has unnecessarily and unreasonably misrepresented them. It has not allowed them to speak to us. Surely it is time for that to change.

## Seeing ourselves from a new perspective

We have all become familiar with the idea of the "neighbour from hell", but we are fairly slow to realise that this might be what we have become. When Jesus was asked about neighbours he intentionally turned the question around. "Who is my neighbour" (Luke 10:29) assumes a passive position. The answer Jesus gave, "Who was a neighbour to the man..." reframed it, asking "What is my relationship with those I find myself alongside?" It takes us, as it took his original interlocutor, from a passive role to one with responsibility. What, for example, do animals across the UK experience on Bonfire Night? What have we done by stretching strips of tarmac in a web that enmeshes and divides the whole land mass without any thought to natural movement and migration? What do we embody when we talk of "owning" animals or land? What do we sweep aside when we call a living being "it" and speak of ourselves as if we exist in isolation?

This is all about what we *value* and what we *ignore*. It is about the stories we weave, which include those we have inherited, woven by former generations who worked with the materials,

185

the knowledge, they had. Whatever we may say about them we cannot claim ignorance ourselves, and it is clear that the story we tell, the very way we understand ourselves, has to change. It is already clear that the old story is instrumental in bringing disaster upon us.

But this is not going to turn into an essay on climate change. The facts about that are well rehearsed elsewhere (see further reading). What I want to focus upon is the positive future, because the story we have told to ourselves about ourselves is incomplete, inaccurate and inhospitable. It is incomplete because it leaves out those with whom our lives are intricately bound; inaccurate because it misses the basic but obvious reality that we cannot exist without nature, and are indeed a part of nature; and inhospitable because the outworking of it is indifference to most and outright hostility to many, and actually does violence to ourselves thereby. It is a story – really a complex of interrelated stories – that has served our wrongly perceived short term needs and desires at the cost of vital long term relationships. Now it is time for that story to be gathered into a greater story, a more life-giving story, which will result in a happier, healthier and altogether more beautiful existence for us all. It is not a narrative that neglects humanity or makes us a disease that needs to be cured. It is one that reconnects us to the elements and the creatures with whom we share the earth, which encompasses other species, the poorest human communities and future generations. It is a story that restores the relationship between women and men across cultures and teaches us to flow with the current of our own nature, recognising our capacity to destroy as well as create and discovering that it is more than ok to be who we are.

So what does this look like in practice? There are, I believe a number of things we can focus upon. Perhaps you will think of others, but here are mine:

## A new centre

As a child I knew instinctively that the world is alive and that I was part of it. As I grew, the culture in which I lived drew me away from that intrinsic knowledge, treated my love of other creatures as a natural childhood naivety, selectively confronted me with 'realities' about human requirements and tried to push me towards human needs and interests. But then I became a Christian. My world view shifted back away from one that was anthropocentric to one where the centre is... well, not us.

A universe whose 'centre' is God finds itself curiously endowed, for the God of Christian faith is not self-centred but is revealed in perfect self-giving, perfect service. Taking the form of part of the creation, the life of Jesus is given away on a lonely cross and restored, and so the will of God is revealed: that we may have life, and have it to the full. But 'we' is not just human beings. The unfolding revelation of the Bible has as one of its threads the love of God of all that is made, the desire of God that all may be one. And so we can say, "everything is alive, everything is sacred, everything is connected, everything is person"[114] and "everything is held".[115]

## Ownership and use

It was when I had nearly finished the book, and was researching Hermit Crab, that I first had to confront the problem of pets head on. I was shocked at how hard it was to find websites that are not about keeping Hermit Crabs. I owe a debt of thanks to the University of Michigan, whose *Animal Diversity Web* website provided most of the information for that chapter,[116] not least because it was encouraging to see that there are extensive studies of this species aimed at moving away from human entertainment towards proper understanding. In the course of writing this I find my belief that trapping wild animals for pets is unacceptable has hardened, and I have determined not to use any information provided by that trade for this publication.

There is a general principle here that bears some prayerful consideration: what are we doing when we seek to own an animal? Some creatures are better suited to domestication than others, but the assumption that we should be able simply to purchase whatever – whoever – we want, like those who go to slave markets, is not in keeping with our calling. Whatever we do has an impact. Whatever we purchase supports a trade. I am not entirely against domestic animals, in fact we keep chickens, but I do believe we have a responsibility towards them. Apart from anything else we do well to consider – depending on the creature – what the impact on our neighbourhood will be. Domestic cats, for example, are intensely territorial. It is humans that force them into such close proximity and this causes them stress. It also has a clear impact upon local habitats. Introducing non-native predators in huge numbers and giving them the advantages of regular food, secure housing and veterinary care cannot fail to. So whilst I recognise the value of animals working with humans in some contexts, I would like to see a wider reflection about how individual rights can result in unintentional damage, and how we might generously forego personal satisfaction for the sake of the community to which we belong. It may even be that we can begin to think of imaginative alternatives to the individualistic, consumer-driven approach that has held sway for so long. We are nothing if not imaginative, and have a great gift of working together, about which more in a moment.

## Thinking together about life together

One of the less appealing aspects of the green movement has been our tendency to focus on personal sacrifice for the sake of a better life. This may be significant to Christians but it does not play well with most people, even giving rise to a comment from someone very close to me about "hair-shirted environmentalists". I can see why that image easily comes to mind, but I do not believe it is accurate or particularly helpful. The goal is not to limit enjoyment but to live fully. In the short-term this can mean letting some things go that we presently enjoy. In a lot of cases I believe abstinence from, say, air travel or meat consumption are important short-term measures that enable sustainable long-term solutions to be found. The debate among environmentalists about the use of nuclear power is another case in point. If we are to have sensible policies that lead to a healthy life for all – and for me that means neighbourhoods that are far richer in wildlife than is presently the case – the conversation needs to involve everyone. It may be ok for some groups of families to have (for example) a cat between them, but what is becoming ever clearer is that the deregulated free market does not deliver a sustainable life, and the losers are those who already have little enough. As some resources, such as oil, become scarcer we will have to adapt. I believe one way to do that will be to move away from individualism and the nuclear family towards small communities who share resources, generate some of their own electricity, grow a lot of their own food and recover a sense of the living world of which they will be a part. I hope therefore that it is clear I do not have a downer on cats *per se*, but rather the culture that has led to the situation we are now in. Like all of us, *Felis silvestris catus* is part of a much bigger picture.

## Welcoming the stranger

Somehow we have become strangers to the world, and the world is strange to us. It is in this context, this fragmentation, that Jesus comes as a stranger (John 1:26), someone who is to be discovered, rather than a familiar figure who exists only to confirm our prejudices. In fact Jesus' ministry, now as then, crucially disappoints us. In doing so he invites us to examine our expectations and desires and realise that there is more to life than *our* life, more to the world than humanity. The wonderful capacity we have to step outside of ourselves and take a cool and knowledgeable look at what we are up to puts us alongside Jesus as he looks upon us. "Have you considered my servant Dan?" he says to me, and we both look on as Dan busies about doing what Dan does.

And the same Jesus also suggests we turn away. "Let's not get too preoccupied with Dan," he suggests, displaying a confidence in me that is immediately reassuring, "Have you considered this Badger, this Ivy, this Ant, this Mushroom? Each expresses in her or his own unique way something of me. Together they reflect an incredible creativity, diversity, life in all its fulness". This touches on an idea I have been living with since autumn 2013,[117] that the belief that we bear the image of God (Genesis 1:27) does not make us superior to other creatures – something I was told in childhood but which is never said in Scripture – but rather calls us to serve them. This goes beyond "stewardship", which still carries the implication that we are in control. We know we are not in control. The image of God in us moves us to love creation and this love is modelled by Jesus not through domination but through service (Matthew 20:28, Mark 10:45). Why we feel the need to be the "crown of all creation" (Anglican Eucharistic Prayer G)[118] is anyone's guess. To me it suggests a certain insecurity. I would like to suggest, then, that we recognise our insecurity, but instead of trying to escape it, treating it as a problem, we embrace it.

## A healthy insecurity

For far too long we have lived out of a need to be on the top perch, although not every human tribe exhibits this. It seems to be mainly a product of a capitalist/consumerist drive. Somehow, though, that drive has proved to be massively popular. In the developed nations we experience some of the knock-on effects: a loss of biodiversity, stress-related health issues, the lack of imaginative play in childhood and so on, but none of that stops others in the world wanting to "catch up". I would like to suggest that as we have become increasingly aware of the bigger picture – the fact of the global biosphere and the effect that human industry is having upon it – there is an invitation from Christ to step down from this lofty yet precarious position and recognise some of our own limits. This recognition does not prevent us from achieving great things, there is no conflict, but it does keep us from foolhardy excess that will not profit us in the long run.

The story of Babel Tower is unusual because in it we hear how God thwarts the first major human project because otherwise "nothing that they propose to do will now be impossible for them" (Genesis 11:6, NRSV). We are not told why this is a problem for God. Could it be that God is afraid? Whatever the motivation, God sows division and confusion and the Tower project is abandoned, crumbling to dust. The site of this, according to the early writers, is the ancient city of Babylon and for more than a thousand years Babylon was an icon in the minds of the people of the Bible, representing human hubris. But what troubled me for many years in my own faith journey was that God could be so petty, acting in a way that seems ignoble, fearful and self-serving. But on retreat in 2003, meditating on this story, I came to realise how well-founded the fear of God is. We have the capacity to destroy our planet many times over. When I was growing up the attention was on the weapons of mass destruction that the cold war antagonists had trained on one another. That threat seems to have largely passed away (although some still cling desperately to the idea of an "independent nuclear deterrent"), but human destruction of the planet goes on apace, and human industry is the cause of it. The Tower continues to rise, and perhaps it is God-in-us that is feeling the fear.

## A living universe
The way Brown Trout and Grayling coexist; the way individuals in a species will work to avoid unnecessary violence; the interdependence of predator and prey; a similar interdependence

between parasite and host; the importance of succession, and of decay; the fact of symbiosis... all these raise for me a big question: we are in the habit of speaking as if things depend essentially upon *competition*. Around the time of writing I even heard a nuclear physicist talking about competition at the sub-atomic level. I would contend that this is one of the more pernicious examples of anthropocentrism. Competition is a purely human concept, because we are the only ones who think in terms of "winners" and "losers". The natural world seems to be far more about relationship and cooperation, interdependence and connection. I would like to suggest that all this is pointing to something we in the Church call "communion". Not the ritual meal that takes place on a regular basis in so many denominations, but a real unity of the cosmos.

*If we live by the Spirit, let us also be guided by the Spirit. Let us not become conceited, competing against one another, envying one another.*
– Galatians 5:25-26 (NRSV)

These words, written to one of the early Christ communities, urged them in the spirit of the teaching of Jesus to love one another (John 13:34-35). The purpose was to be a sign to the human world of the unity that is God's will for the whole of creation (Galatians 3:8). Of course we can say that not all competition is a bad thing, but those examples where competition is healthy – I am thinking particularly of competitive sport – actually require a great deal more cooperation than competition. After all, we cannot compete unless we agree upon the rules and work together with a huge number of others to make the games possible. So where competition exists for good there is always more cooperation. Where it exists in an unhealthy, imbalanced way, such as competition for the world's resources, where cooperation is lacking, it shows itself to be a completely inappropriate model even for human relations. How much more out of place it is then when we consider other species and future generations. The idea of the world as a great competition suits those who benefit from our competitive global system, but if we see the world another way – as a single organism, much like each of us – then just as the cells of your body do not compete for oxygen but rather the blood distributes it to all, so it is with the organism called Earth. Every part has a place. We are blessed in that we are able to see this incredible unity, and the diversity and complexity that sustain it. And with that blessing comes a vital task: to learn how to inhabit it well and truly express the loving creativity, the communion, of the Creator who has chosen it – who has indeed chosen us – to be his temple, his dwelling place.

## Sing a new song

All of this suggests that we need to take a fresh look at ourselves, to come up with a new self-understanding, a new story about who we are. We all live with a collection of stories. The thing to be aware of is that stories are selective: they are constructed out of the information we choose and shaped by what information we leave out. For far too long we have told a story in which humans live in a kind of vacuum. Even (especially?) those who want to see a greater "spiritual" dimension to life have been guilty of this. So much so-called spirituality has been about shutting the world out, going into a room, shutting oneself off. But spirit is not the opposite of body.

There is a growing community of people who are beginning to sing a new song to the Lord, who are learning to live in tune with the earth, in time with her rhythms. They are coming from many different places and perspectives, beginning with their own special interest and finding that it leads them into this greater picture. Like tributaries becoming one river, increasing numbers are aware of an inner urge to know and be known by the life of which we are a part. Institutional religion has not benefitted from this because it is, not without reason, perceived as part of the problem. But for those who are responding to this inner urge faith is important because it has to do with story. They are beginning to discover what might sound at first to be a kind of heresy: that God indwells the *whole* of nature, not just some members of one species. And yet there is not really anything surprising about this. Why would God create a cosmos and then refuse to inhabit it, existing somewhere "outside"? There is nowhere where God is not present, and all things are in God. The argument is not about whether God exists, because there is no category "existence" that God has to conform to. God defines existence. We might even go so far as to say God *is* existence. God is being. I do not mean by this that God has no individuality. Quite the opposite, I believe God continually chooses to indwell the creation, and it is God's presence that gives creation life. When we realise this we begin to understand more fully that humanity is part of the "body" which is nature, a reality that is echoed by the way that Christians make up the "body" which is the Church. The smaller reality (Church) is called to be a sign of the greater reality (Nature) and exists to call people to participate. The ancient call resonates throughout the centuries: choose life.[119] There is no other Way.

# Notes

1.  "Christianity" and "Christian" mean different things to different people. There probably is no neutral term, completely free from unhelpful associations. I wish to locate myself within the global movement of those who follow Jesus Christ, and sit a little more lightly to some of the emphases of institutional church. This is not to deny the central tenets of the tradition, but to be aware that some things that some members of the Church pronounce upon are not of first importance.

2.  George Bernard Shaw originally said this to describe the cultural relationship between the United Kingdom and the United States, but it is a feature of most debates that, despite using the same words antagonists are often appealing to different definitions.

3.  See further reading.

4.  Personal conversation at the first National Forest Church Gathering at Lenchwood Christian Centre, near Evesham, August 2014.

5.  G.K. Chesterton once wrote that the command to love neighbour and enemy are given because often the two are the same! But whenever we identify someone or something or someone as "enemy" it is amazing how it/they then seem to be with us continually. Perhaps this is more about our choice than their action.

6.  http://www.theguardian.com/environment/2014/apr/30/ash-dieback-trees-2018

7.  http://www.forestry.gov.uk/chalara

8.  http://www.dspca.ie/media/badgerbaiting1.pdf

9.  I am grateful to the BBC's *Springwatch* programme for most of the information in this chapter http://www.bbc.co.uk/nature/life/European_Badger

10. NHS Trusts, for example, tend to favour short course Cognitive Behavioural Therapy (CBT) rather than other forms of talking therapy because it focuses on specific outcomes in a short time and therefore accounts for more patients. This looks good on paper and keeps politicians happy, but I would question whether 'productivity' is something that ought to play such a significant role in human well-being.

11. http://www.pure-spirit.com/more-animal-symbolism/651-badger-symbolism

12. Our tendency to divide territory by drawing lines on maps has caused no end of trouble on a human scale throughout history.

13. At the time of writing, action on rewilding seems to be rather slight, but see http://www.wildernessfoundation.org.uk/what-we-do/wilderness-action/wild-britain/

14. The UK Government in 2013 seemed bent on persecuting badgers no matter what, ignoring the advice of scientists in a bid to keep larger landowners happy. http://www.monbiot.com/2010/11/15/spreading-the-white-plague/

15. More information can be gathered from the Badger Trust http://badgertrust.org.uk/

16. http://www.allaboutbirds.org/guide/common_raven/id

17. http://www.garden-birds.co.uk/birds/raven.htm

18. http://www.rspb.org.uk/

19. http://norse-mythology.org/gods-and-creatures/others/hugin-and-munin/

20. http://www.birdguides.com/webzine/article.asp?a=1950

21. http://biblehub.com/topical/r/raven.htm

22. https://www.churchofengland.org/media/1917383/cdm%202003%20as%20amended%20by%20cd(a)m%20july%202013.pdf – see section 8 and https://www.churchofengland.org/about-us/structure/churchlawlegis/clergydiscipline/declarations-under-section-8.aspx

23. I'm grateful to the Revd Paul Cudby of Ancient Arden Forest Church for reminding me of this by posting it on Facebook the day I wrote this chapter in October 2014.

24. http://blog.oup.com/2012/02/mushroom-meaning-life/

25. Jennings, Terry (1987), 'Intelligent Terry's natural knowhow', in BBC Wildlife Magazine vol. 5 no.3, March 1987, p.108.

26. http://tolkiengateway.net/wiki/Gift_of_Men

27. Drane, John et al (2001), Beyond Prediction: The Tarot and Your Spirituality (Oxford: Lion Publishing), pp.69-72 ISBN 0745950353.

28. https://www.gov.uk/guidance/wild-birds-protection-surveys-and-licences

29. https://www.sciencenews.org/blog/wild-things/magpies-don%E2%80%99t-shiny-things

30. http://www.rspb.org.uk/discoverandenjoynature/disco verandlearn/birdguide/name/m/magpie/effect_on_songbird s.aspx

31. Jonathan Gadsby, personal conversation, autumn 2014.

32. http://www.rspb.org.uk I expect those who know about public campaigning would tell me that it is good politics to make people feel that they play a significant role.

33. http://www.mammal.org.uk/species-factsheets/Water %20vole

34. http://www.nottinghamshirewildlife.org/animal-facts/water -vole

35. http://www.bbc.co.uk/news/uk-england-essex-29629264

36. See for example http://www.snh.gov.uk/about-scotlands-nature/species/mammals/land-mammals/water-voles/

37. https://www.goodreads.com/author/quotes/5255891.Ste ve_Jobs

38. http://www.norfolkbiodiversity.org/pdf/biodiversity forum/PoolFrogReintroduction.pdf

39. Tim Minchin's speech to graduates at the University of

Western Australia in 2003. There was a great deal more in this speech that rang true for me than this one point. Indeed there was so much that I agreed with, despite our clear differences of faith that I will almost certainly return to it in a later publication. Watch it if you can. It is only 18 minutes long. http://www.youtube.com/watch?v=yoEezZD71sc

40. http://www.mammal.org.uk/species-factsheets/Common%20shrew

41. Scripture quotation from THE MESSAGE. Copyright © by Eugene H. Peterson 1993, 1994, 1995, 1996, 2000, 2001, 2002. Used by permission of Tyndale House Publishers, Inc.

42. http://www.rspb.org.uk/discoverandenjoynature/discoverandlearn/birdguide/name/b/blackbird/index.aspx

43. Crawford (2009), pp.109, 111. See further reading.

44. http://www.bds.org.uk/

45. http://www.ukbutterflies.co.uk/species.php?vernacular_name=High%20Brown%20Fritillary and http://butterfly-conservation.org/679-985/high-brown-fritillary.html

46. http://www.ignatianspirituality.com/8078/prayer-of-theilhard-de-chardin/

47. http://ngm.nationalgeographic.com/2014/08/neolithic-orkney/brodgar-graphic

48. I am grateful to the Revd David Runcorn for this insight.

49. Skene, Keith, Nature Unleashed: The Meaning of Dominion and our Stewardship of Planet Earth, Recorded at Greenbelt 2012: Eden, 25 Aug 2012, 3.30pm.

50. Any plant that naturally survives through more than one growing season, producing a new crop of seeds each year is called "perennial", whilst "annual" plants survive only long enough to set seed once.

51. Where it says "sat" or "sitting" in the reading it refers to the first-century practice of reclining on rugs and cushions on the floor. The food would be arranged centrally on a board.

52. http://www.woodlandtrust.org.uk/news/latest/lets-cele

brate-mistletoe/

53. http://www.british.mistletoe.org.uk/
54. http://news.nationalgeographic.com/news/2007/12/071224-mistletoe-research.html
55. http://mistletoe.org.uk/infosheets/MistletoeMarblefacts heet.pdf. Another miner is the Mistletoe Weevil, but this is an exotic species, arriving in Britain in 2000.
56. http://news.nationalgeographic.com/news/2007/12/071224-mistletoe-research_2.html
57. http://www.economist.com/node/21558551
58. http://www.orchardnetwork.org.uk/content/mistletoe-campaign
59. http://www.tenburymistletoe.org/festival.html
60. John Drane (200) explores this theme in more depth, pp.101-110 (see further reading).
61. http://www.bats.org.uk/pages/bats_as_indicators.html
62. Stebbings, Bob (1987) "Bats, Tequila and the King of Siam" in *BBC Wildlife* Vol.5 No.1 January 1987, pp.4-8. This was, of course, a completely different species – Tadarida plicata – but the principle is the same.
63. Mexico's Agave Cactus, Indonesia's Durian, African Baobab and Balsa trees. *Ibid.*
64. http://www.sussex.ac.uk/broadcast/read/19003. Unfortunately, honey with too much ivy nectar in it crystallises very quickly, making it hard for Bees to make proper use of it. Beekeepers find it almost impossible to extract from their frames and, to cap it all the flavour is not that great. http://www.garthallan.co.uk/honey.htm
65. Clark, Michael (1987), 'New Moon: February', in *BBC Wildlife* Vol.5 No.2 February 1987, p.68.
66. http://www.tarotforum.net/showthread.php?t=133447
67. http://www.aslsp.org/de/das-projekt.html
68. Ogham is an ancient form of writing used in Ireland. The earliest examples we have are from the 4th Century AD,

although some believe it to be at least three hundred years older. The shapes of the letters are quite tree-like, although scholars believe that ascribing these letters to trees came later on.

69. http://www.woodlandtrust.org.uk/learn/british-trees/native-trees/hawthorn/

70. Dee, Jonathan (2007), *The Runes: An Illustrated Guide to Interpreting the Stones* (Singapore: King Books), pp.43f.

71. Warwick, H. (2008), *A Prickly Affair: My Life with Hedgehogs*, Penguin.

72. http://www.onekind.org/be_inspired/animals_a_z/hedgehog/

73. Anonymous (2015), *Natures Home* (RSPB members' magazine), Autumn 2015, p.14.

74. Hughes, Gerard (1985) *God of Surprises*, (London: DLT).

75. Griffiths, Jay, (2006) *Wild: An Elemental Journey*, (London: Penguin).

76. Greenoak, F. (1979), *All the birds of the air: the names, lore and literature of British birds* (London: Book Club Associates). Quoted by http://www.arkive.org/jay/garrulus-glandarius/

77. http://www.garden-birds.co.uk/birds/jay.htm

78. A bit of folklore: a pest controller (yes I'm afraid so, but I didn't use him) told me that the males tunnel in straight lines whilst females' tunnelling pattern is more random. He used this as a platform for the kind of unnecessary comment about differences between men and women I want to discourage (see the chapter on Deer).

79. I am grateful to Howard Rheingold for this concept. Rheingold, Howard (2012) *Netsmart: How to Thrive Online* (London: MIT Press), pp.148, 149, 157.

80. Parke, Simon (2011) *Solitude: Recovering the power of alone* (Hove: White Crow) http://simonparke.com/books/page/solitude/

81. On 27th February 380

82. Bonhoeffer, Dietrich (1939), *Life Together*, (London: HarperCollins).

83. These are not misspellings. They come from a model of human preferences called the Myers-Briggs Type Indicator. In brief Intra- or Extra-version has to do with how you draw energy. A simple test is to ask what you would do with a free day? Would you go for a long, solitary walk or try to meet up with a friend or friends?

84. I have not been able to trace the source of this by the time of going to print.

85. Eve, Alison, 'The Sacred Circle: Elements of Ritual' in Stanley and Hollinghurst (2014), pp.263-4. See further reading.

86. http://www.ispotnature.org/species-dictionaries/uksi/Eph emera%20danica

87. Willis, Jeanne (2006) *Mayfly Day*, (London: Andersen).

88. See for example http://io9.com/5815582/mayflies-might-just-have-the-saddest-most-perfectly-evolved-existence-of-any-species

89. http://www.bumblebee.org/invertebrates/Ephemeropt era.htm

90. http://www.nhm.org/site/research-collections/mineral-sciences/faqs

91. See further reading. Paul's chapter is on pp.210-227.

92. Harvey, Graham (2005), *Animism: Respecting the Living World* (London: Hurst & Co), p.103.

93. Drane, John (2000) pp.31, 69-70, 125, 173, 176 points out that non-rational is not the same as irrational. See further reading.

94. http://www.foxproject.org.uk/deterrence/

95. http://www.bbc.co.uk/gloucestershire/content/articles /2008/03/31/rob_ward_snakes_feature.shtml

96. See websites.

97. https://www.youtube.com/watch?v=D28X0eLBk3Q

98. This sentence, lifted from the BBC Radio 4 Programme *The Moral Maze*, broadcast on 25th October 2014 (the very day I wrote this chapter), captures exactly the point even though I quote it here out of context. It was said by Psychologist Dr Nina Burrows. http://www.bbc.co.uk/programmes/b04ls mhx at 28 mins 34 seconds.

99. https://www.rhs.org.uk/advice/profile?PID=98

100. Apparently it freezes well too http://www.mushroom diary.co.uk/2013/07/chicken-of-the-woods-bracket-fungus/

101. http://whc.unesco.org/en/list/33

102. This chapter was written immediately after I wrote the one on Kingfisher.

103. From 19 to 65 years in humans. This refers to Erickson's Psychosocial Stages of human life. There are, of course, other models. Stevens, Richard (1983) *Erik Erikson: An Introduction* (New York: St. Martin's).

104. http://themelissagarden.com/TMG_Vetaley031608.htm

105. http://www.whychristmas.com/customs/yulelog.shtml

106. http://www.bbc.com/news/health-10838343

107. http://www.ons.gov.uk/ons/rel/lifetables/historic-and-projected-data-from-the-period-and-cohort-life-tables/2012-based/sty-babies-living-to-100.html

108. Anthony of Egypt, http://www.fatherpius.littleway.ca/desert02.html, quoted in Williams, Rowan (2003) *Silence and Honey Cakes: The Wisdom Of The Desert*, (Oxford: Lion).

109. http://www.mba.ac.uk/learningzone/sealifeinfo/species/crabs/ There are over a thousand species of hermit crabs worldwide.

110. http://www.mcsuk.org/downloads/mcs/MCS_seashore_safari_guide.pdf

111. Two species dominate in the Sargasso Sea, neither of which is the troublesome "Strangleweed", also called "Japanese Wireweed", (*S. muticum*) that occurs on coasts.

112. See further reading.

113. http://www.zsl.org/conservation/regions/uk-europe/eel-conservation
114. http://www.christiananimism.com/
115. Julian of Norwich (trans. Clifton Wolters, 1988), *Revelations of Divine Love*, (London: Penguin) Chapter 5, p.68.
116. http://animaldiversity.ummz.umich.edu/accounts/Pagu rus_bernhardus/
117. When I was invited to contribute to a collection of essays entitled *"Earthed: Christian Perspectives on Nature Connection"* – see further reading.
118. https://www.churchofengland.org/prayer-worship/wor ship/texts/principal-services/holy-communion/epsforone-front/prayerg.aspx
119. I am relieved that I wrote this before reading Alastair McIntosh's inspiring book *Soil and Soul* (p.116, see Further Reading), but also deeply encouraged that this message is being voiced in many places, a sign that this is not just a minority interest but a genuine work of God.

# Websites and further reading

I am grateful to a number of websites and individuals who have assisted me in my research. I have done my best to be original and have sought to avoid plagiarism, but I am aware that others have done some of the same kind of work in their own spheres and that means there may be some overlap.

## Websites

**Alastair McIntosh** teaches an MSc in Spiritual Activism and is the author of *Soil and Soul* (see books below).
*alastairmcintosh.com*

**Beneficials in the Garden** demystifies a large number of creatures in the USA that most gardeners treat as enemies without a second thought. Some of them are found in the UK as well, but it is the approach that is of real value.
*aggie-horticulture.tamu.edu/galveston/beneficials/index.htm*

**Christian Animism** is one of the most unexpected and yet vital developments in Christian faith and practice, which has only begun to be properly articulated in the last couple of years.
*christiananimism.com*

**Communities of the Mystic Christ** is a hub for different groups and individuals who are "interested in exploring Jesus the Christ as a living reality and mystical guide through ancient practices and contemporary thought and experience". The Forest Church movement is probably the most prolific of these and this is where to find out more about it.
*mysticchrist.co.uk*

**The Fox Project** is a charity based in the South East of England, dedicated to providing accurate information about red foxes and how we can live in greater harmony with them.
*foxproject.org.uk*

**The National Amphibian and Reptile Recording Scheme**

(NARRS) has been in existence since 2007 and attempts to monitor the conservation status of all UK amphibian and reptile species. It is a great first port of call for information, and provides opportunities for those who want to assist in data gathering about some of our lesser known native wildlife. *narrs.org.uk/index.php*

**The National Hedgelaying Society** may sound geeky, but you cannot hope for an activity that better links your health to that of the land. *hedgelaying.org.uk*

**Pure Spirit** is the business website of Marilyn Tokach, who seeks greater understanding between people and animals. *pure-spirit.com*

**Slug Off** and **Slug Watch** The very fact that these websites exist at all is gratifying. Two whole websites just about slugs. Who would have thought it? *slugoff.co.uk* and *slugwatch.co.uk*

**The Wilderness Foundation** "Our vision is a world where the well-being of people, species and wild places are in balance". *www.wildernessfoundation.org.uk*

**The Wildlife Trusts** are active in conservation and education. They are particularly family-friendly and local in the way they work and have important connections with local authorities. *wildlifetrusts.org*

**Wild About Food** provides a good introductory guide to foraging, preparing and preserving wild food. They also run events and workshops and sell food made from foraged ingredients. *wildaboutfood.co.uk*

**Wild About Gardens** is a collaboration between the Wildlife Trusts and the Royal Horticultural Society. It includes ideas about wildlife-friendly gardening and information about some species you may encounter in your own backyard. *wildaboutgardens.org.uk*

**Wild England** aims to provide information on 365 species native to England. Categorizing the pages by school year means that this will be an excellent resource for anyone who wants to encourage their children to develop their understanding of our native wildlife. *wildengland.com*

Other websites I used to gather general information for this book:

a-z-animals.com
allaboutbirds.org
allaboutfrogs.org
animaldiversity.org (University of Michigan)
arkive.org
badgertrust.org.uk
bats.org.uk
bbc.com/earth/uk
bbc.co.uk/nature/life/
bds.org.uk (British Deer Society)
birdguides.com
birdinginformation.com
britannica.com
britishcountryside.webplus.net (Offwell Woodland and Wildlife
    Trust, Devon)
british.mistletoe.org.uk
bumblebee.org
butterfly-conservation.org
encyclopedia.com
first-nature.com
forestry.gov.uk (Forestry Commission)
froglife.org
garden-birds.co.uk
herpetofauna.co.uk
ignatianspirituality.com
ispotnature.org
kew.org (Royal Botanical Gardens)
mammal.org.uk (The Mammal Society)

marlin.ac.uk (Marine Life Information Network)

mba.ac.uk (Marine Biological Association of the UK)

mcsuk.org (Marine Conservation Society)

mistletoe.org.uk

mushroomdiary.co.uk

nhm.org (Natural History Museum)

norse-mythology.org

onekind.org (UK based animal protection charity)

opalexplorenature.org (Open Air Laboratories Network)

orchardnetwork.org.uk

paulkirtley.co.uk (Bushcraft Instructor's Blog)

peta.org (People for the Ethical Treatment of Animals)

rspb.org.uk

sttiggywinkles.org.uk (wildlife hospital in Buckinghamshire)

suffolkwildlifetrust.org

sussexotters.org.uk

tenburymistletoe.org

themelissagarden.com

ukbutterflies.co.uk

uksafari.com

whats-your-sign.com

wildtrout.org

woodlandtrust.org.uk

zsl.org (Zoological Society of London)

## Further reading

I have not read all of these, but in most cases I have seen a copy and at least flicked briefly through. If anything below is inaccurate I apologise and take full responsibility.

**Beck, Shawn Sanford (2015),** *Christian Animism* **(Ropley, Hants: Christian Alternative)** dispels the myth that Christianity separates us from connection with nature and encourages a new awareness of the life all around us. ISBN 978-1782799658

**Berry, Wendell (2000),** *Life is a Miracle: An Essay Against Modern Superstition* **(Washington: Counterpoint)** challenges the prevailing mechanistic/reductionist worldview which, he posits, blights all discussion of ecology. Berry calls for a recovery of interrelatedness, mystery and organic language, not only among those hostile to the natural world but also among some of its defenders, in particular the author E.O. Wilson. ISBN 1582431418

**Crawford, Matthew (2009),** *The Case for Working With Your Hands: or Why Office Work is Bad for Us and Fixing Things Feels Good,* **(London: Penguin Viking Books)** Explores the impact of separating 'academic' and 'practical' work and how they might be re-integrated. ISBN 978-0670918744

**Drane, John (2000),** *The McDonaldization of the Church: Spirituality, Creativity, and the Future of the Church* **(London: Darton, Longman and Todd)** Addresses the challenges facing Christianity in postmodern developed societies and proposes a number of ways forward. ISBN 0232522596

**Louv, Richard (2008),** *Last Child in the Woods: Saving Our Children From Nature-Deficit Disorder* **(Chapel Hill, NC: Algonquin Books)** inspired such initiatives as *Project Wild Thing* and the National Trust's *"30 things to do before you are 11 ¾"*. ISBN 978-1565126053

**MacFarlane, Robert (2007),** *The Wild Places* **(London: Granta)** explores parts of Britain in order to recapture an awareness of our wild landscape. In the process the author helpfully challenges some of the ways in which we have become disconnected from the land with which we are – whether we are aware of it or not – intimately connected. ISBN 978-1847080189

**Macfarlane, Robert (2012),** *The Old Ways: A Journey on Foot* **(London: Penguin)** and *The Wild Places* Two inspiring works that question our assumptions about the natural world and invite us to go out and experience nature's strangeness and hospitality for ourselves.

**McIntosh, Alastair (2004),** *Soil and Soul: People versus Corporate Power* **(London: Aurun Press)** "We yearn for connection ... But we forget that, like the earthworm, we too are an organism of the soil". An incredible story of insight and political resistance that gives hope to all humanity. ISBN 978-1-85410-942-2

**Marshall, George (2014),** *Don't Even Think About It: Why Our Brains Are Wired To Ignore Climate Change* **(London: Bloomsbury Press)** Unearths the strange internal transactions that mean we accept the facts about climate change and then, perilously, do nothing about it. ISBN 978-1-6204013-3-0

**Monbiot, George (2014),** *Feral: Rewilding the Land, Sea and Human Life* **(London: Penguin)**
An exploration of rewilding by an author who rigorously cites all his sources and builds a convincing argument for something that is already meeting fierce resistance. ISBN 978-0-1419755-8-0

**Semlyen, Anna,** *Cutting Your Car Use: Save Money, be Healthy, be Green* **(Cambridge: Green Books, 2007)** with illustrations by Axel Scheffler, this is a short, practical guide that helps you do what it says on the cover. ISBN 978-1-900322157

**Sheldrake, Rupert (1990),** *The Rebirth of Nature: The Greening of Science and God* **(Rochester, Vermont: Park Street Press)**
Traces some of the history of our disconnection with nature and proposes a rejection of a mechanistic understanding of the

universe in favour of seeing nature as alive. Explores morphic field theory and respects historic faith perspectives without assuming anything uncritically. ISBN 978-1-6205504-9-6

**Stanley, Bruce (2013), *Forest Church: A field guide to nature connection for groups and individuals* (Llangurig, Powys: Mystic Christ Press)**
The first book written about this emerging movement, exploring how an individual might approach the subject and possibly facilitate a group. Includes an extensive bibliography, helpfully grouped by subject, to enable readers to follow up their own areas of interest. ISBN 978-0-9575383-0-6

**Stanley, B and Hollinghurst, S (eds) (2014), *Earthed: Christian Perspectives on Nature Connection* (Llangurig: Mystic Christ Press)**
A series of essays by those involved with Forest Church groups in different parts of the country (includes my chapter, *Rewilding the Soul*). ISBN 978-0-9575383-2-0

**Warwick, H. (2012), *The Beauty in the Beast: Britain's Favourite Creatures and the People Who Love Them*, (London: Simon & Schuster)**
The author considers fifteen species and some of the people who study them. Like this book, his aim is to help the reader fall in love with nature and develop that love affair through directly encountering the life that is all around us. ISBN 978-0857203953

# Scripture Index

Genesis 1:27 Conclusions, 190

Genesis 2:7 Adder, 159

**Genesis 2:9 Ash, 9**

Genesis 3:1-15 Adder, 159

Genesis 4:9 Rook, 31

Genesis 8:7 Raven, 20

Genesis 11:6 Conclusions, 191

**Exodus 3:2-3, 5-6 Red Ant, 12**

Leviticus 11:13, 15 Raven, 20

Numbers 21:4-9 Adder, 162

Numbers 22:26-34 Fox, 152

**Numbers 24:3-4, 17 Magpie, 41**

**Deuteronomy 6:5-7 Badger, 16**

Deuteronomy 30:19 Conclusions, 194

Judges 7:2-7 Raven, 21

**1 Kings 2:1-3, 5-6, 8-9 St Georges Mushroom, 26**

**1 Kings 17:2-4 Raven, 20**

1 Kings 19:5-8 Raven, 21

Job 8:11-14 Common Orb Weaver, 144

**Job 12:7-10 Brown Trout, 36**

Job 38:41 Raven, 20

**Job 39:26-30 Peregrine, 45**

Psalms 19, Introduction, 5

Psalm 24:1 Mole, 131

Psalm 27:14 High Brown Fritillary, 71

**Psalm 33:4-6, 20-22 Common**

**Frog, 52**

Psalm 96:1 Trees, Conclusion, 115, 193

Psalm 98:1 Conclusion, 193

Psalm 98:3 Raven, 21

Psalms 104 Introduction, 5

Psalm 118 St George's Mushroom, 28

Psalm 127:1 Blackbird, 61

**Psalm 131 Water Vole, 48**

Psalm 147:9 Raven, 20

Psalm 148 Introduction, 5

Psalm 150:6 Raven, 21

Proverbs 30:25 Red Ant, 11

Proverbs 30:28 Common Orb Weaver, 143

**Ecclesiastes 3:1, 10-13 Blackbird, 59**

**Song of Solomon 1:2-4; 2:3, 6; 4:5-7, 11, 16; 5:4-5, 8 Roe Deer, 65**

Song of Solomon 5:16 Roe Deer, 67

Song of Solomon 6:10 Roe Deer, 66

Isaiah 49:6 Rook, 31

**Isaiah 53:1-3, 10 Shrew, 55**

Isaiah 58:6 Rook, 31

Isaiah 59:5 Common Orb Weaver, 145

Jeremiah 23:24 Raven, 21

Ezekiel 3:17-19 Rook, 31

Ezekiel 37:1, 4-7 High Brown
Fritillary, 70

Jonah 1:1-4, 10-12 Leopard
Slug, 75

Zecheriah 12:10 Adder, 162

Matthew 5:44 Introduction,
Rook, 2, 31

Matthew 6:25 Grey Seal, 102

Matthew 6: 28 Common Frog,
53

Matthew 7:15, 19-20, 21 Honey
Bee, 87

Matthew 9:9-13 Pipistrelle, 91-
2

Matthew 9:10 Rosebay
Willowherb, 80

Matthew 11:2-5, 7, 18-19 Ivy,
95

Matthew 13:24-30 Chicken of
the Woods, 166

Matthew 16:24-28 Grey Seal,
100

Matthew 17:24-27 Red
Squirrel, 105

Matthew 18:1 Mole, 132

Matthew 18:1-5 Toad, 112

Matthew 20:28 Conclusions,
190

Matthew 21:12 Stoat, 109

Matthew 22:39 Introduction, 2

Matthew 23:1-15 Stoat, 108

Mark 2:13-17 Rosebay
Willowherb, 79

Mark 4:2-3, 21, 26, 31, 34
White-berried Mistletoe, 84

Mark 9:14-29 Hawthorn, 118-9

Mark 10:45 Conclusions, 190

Mark 12:31 Introduction, 2

Mark 12:41-44 Jay, 128

Mark 16:15 Raven, 21

Luke 2:32 Rook, 31

Luke 3:21-22 Kingfisher, 137

Luke 5:29 Rosebay
Willowherb, 80

Luke 6:12-16, 20 Mole, 131

Luke 6:27-36 Introduction,
Mayfly, 2, 141

Luke 9:46 Mole, 132

Luke 9:51-53 Kingfisher, 136

Luke 9:57-58 Kingfisher, 136

Luke 9:62 Toad, 113

Luke 10:29 Conclusions, 185

Luke 12:16-18, 20-21, 22, 24,
27-28, 32-34 Common Orb
Weaver, 144

Luke 12:23 Grey Seal, 102

Luke 12:24, 27 Common Frog,
53

Luke 12:50 Kingfisher, 137

Luke 13:31-34 Kingfisher, 137

Luke 19:1-10 Hedgehog, 123

Luke 19:29-30, 36-40
Meteorite, 149

Luke 21:1-4 Jay, 128

Luke 22:24 Mole, 132

John 1:13 Kingfisher, 137

John 1:26 Conclusions, 189

John 2:15 Stoat, 109

John 2:23-24; 6:2, 5-11, 14-15
Fox, 154

John 3:1-3, 14-15 Adder, 161

John 3:1-21 Toad, 112

John 3:8 Common Frog, Toad,
53, 113, 114

John 12:20-32 Jay, 128

John 13:34-35 Conclusions, 192

John 17:1-3, 6, 8, 20-23, 26
Chicken of the Woods, 165-6

John 19:37 Adder, 162

1 Corinthians 1:27 Shrew, 56

1 Corinthians 1:27-28
Kingfisher, 135

1 Corinthians 12:12-15, 17, 21,

26 Oak, 171

2 Corinthians 12:9 Shrew, 56

Galatians 3:8 Conclusions, 192

Galatians 5:22-23 Honey Bee,
88

Galatians 5:25-26 Conclusions,
192

Ephesians 2:11-13; 3:14-19 Eel,
181-2

Colossians 3:3 Hedgehog, 125

Hebrews 13:2 Hedgehog, 122

James 1:18 Raven, 21

James 4:6 Shrew, 56

1 Peter 2:5-10 Hermit Crab,
176

Revelation 22:1-2 Ash, 9

CHRISTIAN
ALTERNATIVE

Throughout the two thousand years of Christian tradition there
have been, and still are, groups and individuals that exist in the
margins and upon the edge of faith. But in Christianity's
contrapuntal history it has often been these outcasts and
pioneers that have forged contemporary orthodoxy out of
former radicalism as belief evolves to engage with and
encompass the ever-changing social and scientific realities. Real
faith lies not in the comfortable certainties of the Orthodox, but
somewhere in a half-glimpsed hinterland on the dirt track to
Emmaus, where the Death of God meets the Resurrection, where
the supernatural Christ meets the historical Jesus, and where the
revolution liberates both the oppressed and the oppressors.

Welcome to Christian Alternative... a space at the edge where
the light shines through.